TRANSCENDENTAL MEDICATION

Transcendental Medication considers why human brains evolved to have consciousness, yet we spend much of our time trying to reduce our awareness. It outlines how limiting consciousness—rather than expanding it—is more functional and satisfying for most people, most of the time.

The suggestion is that our brains evolved mechanisms to deal with the stress of awareness in concert with awareness itself—otherwise it is too costly to handle. Defining dissociation as "partitioning of awareness," Lynn touches on disparate cultural and psychological practices such as religion, drug use, 12-step programs, and dancing. The chapters draw on biological and cultural studies of Pentecostal speaking in tongues and stress, the results of our 800,000+ years watching hearth and campfires, and unconscious uses of self-deception as a mating strategy.

Written in a highly engaging style, *Transcendental Medication* will appeal to students and scholars interested in mind, altered states of consciousness, and evolution. It is particularly suitable for those approaching the issue from cultural, biological, psychological, and cognitive anthropology, as well as evolutionary psychology, cognitive neuroscience, and religious studies.

Christopher D. Lynn is Professor of Anthropology at the University of Alabama, USA. He is co-editor of *Evolution Education in the American South* (2017) and co-host of the *Sausage of Science* and *Inking of Immunity* podcasts.

TRANSCENDENTAL MEDICATION

The Evolution of Mind, Culture, and Healing

Christopher D. Lynn

Routledge
Taylor & Francis Group

LONDON AND NEW YORK

Cover image: © Bruce Rolff / Stocktrek Images / Getty Images

First published 2022
by Routledge
4 Park Square, Milton Park, Abingdon, Oxon OX14 4RN

and by Routledge
605 Third Avenue, New York, NY 10158

Routledge is an imprint of the Taylor & Francis Group, an informa business

© 2022 Christopher D. Lynn

The right of Christopher D. Lynn to be identified as author of this work
has been asserted in accordance with sections 77 and 78 of the Copyright,
Designs and Patents Act 1988.

British Library Cataloguing-in-Publication Data
A catalogue record for this book is available from the British Library

Library of Congress Cataloging-in-Publication Data
A catalog record has been requested for this book

ISBN: 978-0-367-47264-1 (hbk)
ISBN: 978-0-367-47263-4 (pbk)
ISBN: 978-1-003-03448-3 (ebk)

DOI: 10.4324/9781003034483

Typeset in Bembo
by SPi Technologies India Pvt Ltd (Straive)

CONTENTS

PREFACE

Writing a book has been a dream of mine for much longer than I've studied the subject of this one. When I was in my 20s, I thought if I hadn't written a book by the time I was 30, I should quit my job and dedicate myself to my craft like Knut Hamsun's character in *Hunger*.[1] Instead, I went back to college, finished my undergraduate degree and went on to graduate school and got a PhD, started a family, and became a professor. Now, I write as much as I ever wanted to, and yet, it's taken me over ten years into my professional career to realize this particular dream.

The spark finally came from a Human Biology Association workshop where I was told I should have a position paper when I go up for tenure that would outline my integrated research agenda. At the time, I didn't have a position paper or an integrated agenda. Like many first-generation college students, I thought that once I got a job, I could just do research. I looked around and realized that many of my colleagues who write both scholarly papers for fellow experts and books for the public write the position paper first and then expand on that for the book. I started the paper but got tenure without it, and, now, here, I've gone and written the book anyway.

This book's imperfections are all mine, but many people helped me improve it along the way. First, I thank some of the inspirations for insights you will read about, my wife Loretta and my kids Bailey, Lux, and Jagger. Raising a family has been the best training in learning to focus attention and to dissociate from irrelevant distractions, the subjects of this book. As a grad student, having three infants at home and a wife taking care of them all day long by herself is what kept my nose to grindstone, as it were. Even in the midst of emotional breakdowns and stomach viruses, I had toddlers depending on me and keeping me going. Moreover, I can tune out people and things I don't want to face like a pro. Perhaps that is why, during the summer of 2020, the COVID-19 pandemic did not distract me from finishing the draft I sent off to the publisher (though it certainly didn't give me the same motivation during the subsequent year of editing after getting the reviewer comments back). Or maybe it was having the comfort of my family around to reassure me. Regardless, I thank them for suffering me and for their inspiration.

I thank my parents, Eddie and Vicki Lynn, for instilling in me the confidence to do pretty much anything I set my mind to, including being the first person in my family to get a graduate degree and write a book. My sister Brittany Van Meter and our extended family are cut from the same cloth. I have always felt loved and supported, and this is for all of you.

I have many other people to thank for various types of support, from relatively mundane but critical words of encouragement to the reading chapters, pointing out sources, and polishing my writing. A special thank you to people like my close friends and colleagues Cara Ocobock and Lesley Jo Weaver, my in-laws Hank and Pat Jenkins, our dogs (Gallifrey, Sugarfoot, Tiberius, and now Peewee), and my academic advisers Lawrence Schell, Gordon Gallup, Jr., Walter Little, and John Beatty.

I thank my colleagues around the world who responded to queries with sources, gave me ideas, or bolstered my credentials to the higher-ups to get me my job and keep me around, starting with those stuck in Alabama with me: Keith Jacobi, Jason DeCaro, Toni Copeland, Bill Dressler, Kathy Oths, Jim Bindon, Sonya Pritzker, Michael Murphy, Ian Brown, Marysia Galbraith, Courtney Helfrecht, Missy Sartain, and Teri Kirkendoll (RIP). I thank my friends who went through grad school with me and teachers and professors who helped train me everywhere and still support me: Sharon DeWitte, Sean Rafferty, Bria Dunham, Melinda Denham, Julia Ravenscroft, Mia Gallo, Courtney Kurlanska, Jason Paris, Nate Pipitone, Julian Paul Keenan, Cheryl Frye, Glenn Geher, Lee Cronk, Ma Booth, Moustafa Bayoumi, and Roni Natov.

There are a million people I've texted, cornered at a conference, or emailed over the years whose feedback and thoughts are littered throughout these pages, sometimes named and other times not but whose importance in this journey is without question: Bill Leonard, Sara Lewis, Bonnie Kaiser, Rebecca Lester, Jeff Snodgrass, Barbara King, Pat Hawley, Tanya Luhrmann, David Sloan Wilson, Julie Lesnik, Michael Winkelman, Andrew Newberg, Rich Sosis, Bob Trivers, Janet Dixon Keller, Grant Rich, Montserrat Soler, Dan Povinelli, Matt Rossano, Rebecca Seligman, Michaela Howells, Mel Konner, Daniel Lende, Greg Downey, Peter Stromberg, Del Paulhus, John Hawks, and Ben Campbell.

I am grateful to the many current and former students who have worked with me in developing these ideas, several of whom are off doing related work as professors now too: Max Stein, Francois Dengah, Andrew Bishop, Serafina Grottanelli, Lisa Brazelton, Olivia Radcliffe, Avery McNeece, Julia Sponholtz, Laura Ditmore, Erica Schumann, and Dillon Patterson.

I am so appreciative for the brethren of the Triumphant Apostolic Church of Jesus Christ and Abundant Life Tabernacle for their grace in welcoming me among them during my doctoral work and for the hospitality of Melinda Johnson, her kids Winston and Charlie Baylis, and the Church of God of Prophecy in Costa Rica.

I thank my friends whose spirits filter through these pages, sometimes in print and other times just in my mind as I write and tell our stories. These friends have been part of a long voyage and are all mixed up here but represent growing up in Indiana, my music days in NYC, starting my family in the Hudson Valley, and moving to Alabama to raise my family: Brent Colyer (RIP) and his parents Rob (RIP) and Lynne Colyer, Jose Moreno, Scott Dennis, Rusty Floyd, Lou Mansdorf, Maureen and Katie Eiwanger, Tracy Toscano, Liz Bonsal, Loreta Boskovic, Jeff and Kip Smith, Mark Eis, Kelly Horwitz, Rebecca Rothman, Bo Hicks, Jamie Ciciatello, Jahna Rain Balk, Sean Gibbons, Rick Williams, Joni Adams, Brandon Unroe, Kelli Ball, Jill Swan, Anna and Norman (RIP) Singer, and our great Druid Hills neighbors.

I am fortunate to have received funding for the research I discuss in this book from the University of Alabama, Brooklyn College, the University at Albany, the National Science Foundation, and the Society for the Scientific Study of Religion.

Finally, I thank my editors at Routledge, the anonymous reviewers who recommended many good changes and my personal editor and friend Donna Eis who gave me a tissue when the reviews hurt my feelings and who helped me to through them, word by word.

Everyone else who helped me and my family along the way who I have shamefully forgotten at the moment, next book, I swear, I will thank you.

Keep tuning out!

Christopher Lynn
September 14, 2021
Tuscaloosa, Alabama

Note

1 Knut Hamsun, *Hunger* (L. Smithers, 1899).

1

CONSCIOUSNESS AS A BY-PRODUCT

"D'jeet?" and Other Culturally Relative Patterns of Consciousness

My wife and I divide up cooking dinner during the workweek, both hoping the other person will cook on the unclaimed nights. I usually step up because I enjoy cooking, and she decidedly does not. As our kids are teenagers now, with complicated work, sports, school, and social schedules, we are often not all home at the same time. On weekends, the dinner plan is frequently "fend for yourselves." It's not unusual for our kids to sit at their computers gaming for hours on end. Around 9 or 10 p.m., I might ask them, "d'jeet sum'n?", "d'jeet yet?", or merely "d'jeet?"

In context, most Americans would know what this means, despite the fact that none of these phrases is recognizable as grammatically correct English in any country. As linguists like John McWhorter and my undergrad mentor John Beatty point out, our brains rapidly understand and translate these queries as "did you eat something?", "did you eat yet?", and "did you eat?", respectively.[1] The reason we recognize these non-English utterances as words is that they are familiar patterns that trigger motifs in our consciousness. Most of the time, humans can take in multiple sensory sensations and think at the same time, though our consciousness or awareness may be primarily focused on one or a few things. Right now, I hear the sounds of a video game, a buzzing smartphone, a dehumidifier, and the clicking of my son's fingers on his keyboard behind me. At the same time, I am aware of the discomfort of the cheap desk chair I sit in and of the semi-coldness of my feet. I can make sense of all these noises and sensations because I am in a context of maximum familiarity, my own home. "D'jeet?" makes perfect sense in this context in the evening on a weekend. Yet consciousness is relative. In a less familiar environment, I would have to concentrate harder to make sense of the sounds around me and to interpret any words spoken to me.

DOI: 10.4324/9781003034483-1

If something as simple as asking in one's own native tongue if someone has eaten requires such varying degrees of focus on the part of the person being questioned, how can we explain multiple levels of awareness? What happens when our brains are engaged in two or more things simultaneously or in rapid succession, as when an elite American football quarterback calculates where to throw the ball within a field of constantly shifting receivers on his team and opposing players chasing them while scrambling to avoid being tackled? How do I stay focused on writing these words and not attune to the sound of the dryer door that is now opening or my dog stirring behind me? Neuroscientist Nikos Logothetis suggests we can begin to understand the mechanisms of consciousness by breaking it up into sensory parts and examining them independently. In his studies of visual perception in human and non-human primates, he finds that human sensory receptors respond vigorously to preferred or familiar patterns but are physically inhibited when not exposed to preferred stimuli. The more receptors that are stimulated, the greater our awareness of whatever is activating them.[2]

What happens if two stimuli are equally familiar or trigger an equal number of receptors? Probably a bit of chaos. I borrow an experiment from Logothetis to illustrate this idea with regard to visual awareness. Take the cardboard tube from a roll of paper towels and another from a roll of toilet paper. Tape them together to form a pair of binoculars. Place them to your eyes and put a hand over the toilet paper tube opening and look at another object through the paper towel tube. Be sure to keep both eyes open. What generally happens is that your hand is too close to focus on, though you are seeing through both eyes. You are technically seeing two things at once, but since you cannot focus on your hand, the perception from your other eye will dominate. It will appear that you have a hole through your hand. Now, take two paper towel tubes and tape different images at the end of each one. Make sure some light gets through so you can focus on the images. Now you have two different images, one going to each eye. What do you see?

Ordinarily, our visual field is an integration of what our two eyes see. Visual receptors in each eye are connected to nerves that go directly through the eye's respective brain hemisphere to the primary visual cortex at the back of the brain, but also to nerves that cross the corpus callosum (the large bundle of nerves connecting the brain hemispheres), and then proceed to the primary visual cortex. Integration of visual perception then takes place in the brain's secondary association area near the primary visual cortex in conjunction with the raw reception of incoming signals. There are no visual receptors at the spot in our eyes where optic nerves leave the eyeball, but we don't perceive this blind spot. The secondary visual perception areas seamlessly accommodate these gaps by integrating the separate but overlapping fields of vision coming into each eye.

This binocular experiment undermines normal visual integration, an aspect of perception that is common in all primates. The tubes prevent the overlap of what each eye is seeing, regardless of the neural integration that comes afterward. How does our brain make sense of two different simultaneous visual inputs? If you've done this experiment properly—and sometimes it takes playing with things a bit to get the effect just right—you experience a visual toggling. Your brain does not blur them together as one might expect, but switches back and forth, over and over.

Now imagine you are that football quarterback. How do you attune to the stimuli that are important and tune out those that are not? Certainly, the crowd noise is not relevant, and neither is the smack-talking from the players on the other team, though they are trying to get in your head. If you have practiced enough, you automatically weigh your options. For a pass play, you quickly scan your receivers in a specific order to see who is open, being careful not to look at them directly because the defense is watching your eyes to anticipate your throw. For a "run-pass option," you prepare to hand the ball off to a running back, unless it appears the defense is coming for him, in which case you pull the ball back and step around in a pocket created by blockers and then look to throw. Your running back now becomes a blocker, and you scan your receivers for a small window you can throw the ball through. If that option is not available, you tuck it yourself and run through a hole in the offensive and defensive lines of players or to the "edge," toward the sideline. Throughout all of this, you maintain proprioceptive awareness (i.e., of your body in space) of what is around you so that you can avoid tackles. A small step one way or another can change the outcome of the play. We may not see a person getting ready to tackle us, but if our "Spidey-sense" begins tingling, we know it may be time to move.

Human consciousness is optimized specifically for such decision-making. Or, to put it another way, our proprioceptive awareness is the preadaptation we have for consciousness. This awareness of our bodies in relation to our environment is a sort of self-recognition that has also been observed in some other hominid species, though cognitive scientist Daniel Povinelli, who conducted hundreds of experiments on great ape intelligence, working primarily with captive chimpanzees in his University of Louisiana at Lafayette facility during the 1990s and early 2000s, concluded that great apes other than humans possess neither consciousness nor awareness of others the way we think of those capacities.[3]

Interestingly, chimpanzees and orangutans, which are both large-bodied great apes that travel through trees, seem to recognize themselves in mirrors, whereas gorillas, their fellow hominids, do not. (I will return to this topic in more detail in Chapter 3 when I discuss the work of Gordon Gallup Jr. and mirror tests for self-recognition.) This is surprising, as humans are much more closely related to gorillas and chimps—and gorillas and chimps are more closely related to each other—than gorillas, chimps, or humans are to orangutans. Orangutans split off first from a shared common ancestor, then gorillas, then the chimp species (common chimps and bonobos are in the same genus and equally distantly related to us). Thus, from a phylogenetic (or family tree for species) point of view, the ability of orangutans to recognize themselves should have been in the common ancestor and appeared in gorillas too. It would be highly unusual for a trait to disappear and reappear like that, with some exceptions (penile spines, for instance, have evolved and disappeared approximately nine times in primates, but genitals are the nexus of sexual selection and evolve faster than other features).[4]

Human-raised gorillas with substantial enrichment—like the late Koko, a captivity-raised lowland gorilla taught by developmental psychologist Penny Patterson to use American Sign Language as an infant and who reportedly understood as many as 2000 spoken English words—seem to pass modifications of the mirror test for self-recognition. These exceptions suggest that self-recognition of this sort may be a dormant trait in gorillas. Povinelli extends this by suggesting that self-recognition is neurologically expensive and shouldn't manifest unless it is useful.

Gorillas largely stay on the ground and are big enough and live in groups of multiple large males, females, and their offspring and thus do not have to worry about predators. Orangutans are large as well, but the males live alone and females with their offspring, so remain in the trees, likely for protection from each other as much as from potential predation. Most arboreal (tree-living) primates use all four limbs and walk on top of tree branches or swing from branch to branch like the much smaller "lesser" apes called gibbons and siamangs. Orangutans are so big they must distribute their weight among branches. If orangutans fall, the likelihood of getting seriously injured is far greater than for smaller-bodied apes and monkeys. When is it more useful to have a sense and recognition of oneself relative to the environment than when one is a big-bodied furball lumbering through the treetops? Thus, what the mirror test seems to elicit is higher-order proprioceptive awareness or a sense of oneself in space.

Consciousness as a By-Product

The idea that human consciousness is a by-product of biology is not new. Carl Sagan advanced it in his book *Dragons of Eden*, drawing in part on the late neuroscientist Paul Maclean's concept of the triune brain. Maclean hypothesized that the modern vertebrate forebrain evolved by building on the reptilian complex of the basal ganglia, the paleomammalian complex of the limbic system, and the neomammalian complex of the neocortex. The notion of humans exhibiting primitive behavior because of our "reptilian" or "animal" brains seeped into culture throughout the 1970s and 1980s. It is common to hear people refer to our "reptilian brain" when explaining or forgiving behavior that it seems humans should be able to rise above. My kids' principal once dismissed some questionable behavior as typical of "boys' reptilian brains." The principal made a mess of the science, but the ideas underlying the triune brain are part of our culture.[5]

There is little agreement on what human consciousness is or how to define it, but most definitions depend in some way on being aware of internal and external states. The consciousness model outlined in this book can be generalized as constituting three simple but complex related capacities: self-awareness, theory of mind, and dissociation. Self-awareness is the ability to distinguish the self from others and to be able to reflect about oneself vis-à-vis others, while theory of mind is the use of self-awareness to be able to infer the probable mental state of another based on personal experience or knowledge of a similar situation. Therefore, theory of mind presupposes self-awareness. However, no one is either totally self-aware or completely attuned to the minds of those around them, and this is because aware-ness is a burden with high costs. In fact, research on deception-detection suggests that people may not be particularly good at sensing the minds of others, but merely demonstrating empathetic efforts—trying to care about what others think—is often all that is expected of us.[6] Just trying to understand another's perspective goes a long way in social situations, however imperfect we may be at actually understand-ing another's perspective. Signaling our willingness to cooperate or our attempts to be empathetic, may be more necessary from an evolutionary perspective than our accuracy in guessing another's mind. Dissociation is the capacity that reduces the stress of all this higher-order insight and enables humans to manage those costs.

Dissociation Facilitates Transcendence

My wife is a dance-movement therapist and was training for a master's degree at Pratt Institute while I was finishing my undergraduate degree and first became interested in anthropology. Dance-Movement Therapy is a psychoanalytic approach to therapy that focuses on movement integration, and the Pratt program she attended is based in Freudian and Jungian psychoanalysis. The ability of therapists to "read" clients' movements and to help get them moving in rhythmic and group-oriented ways resonated strongly with my anthropological readings, particularly those including cross-cultural Indigenous medical systems revolving around shamanism and pos-session. My wife's master's project involved interpreting video of her clinical work with patients at Woodhull Medical Center in Bedford-Stuyvesant, Brooklyn, in the inpatient psychiatric ward. Bed-Stuy is the fourth poorest neighborhood in the US and has a large immigrant population. Many of the patients were mentally ill, did not speak English as a first language (if at all), and were homeless. Therefore, there were numerous barriers to verbal therapy with these patients.

Watching videos of her sessions with patients in which they would gather around a parachute and use it as a pivot to facilitate group movement led me to two epiphanies: first, the social skills and movement integration that she was facilitating with her patients were the same type of behavior depicted in ethnographic films like Maya Deren's *Divine Horsemen* (about Haitian *Vodou*, or voodoo, by its common name) or John Marshall's *N/um Tchai: The Ceremonial Dance of the !Kung Bushmen*. These films depict shamanic spirit possession and possession trance or what might be more generally called "dissociative trance" or simply "dissociation." Whereas the fulcrum for the activities in the ritual settings of Vodou or !Kung trance dancing is often a fire or something similar, the non-linguistic approach to social integration in these cases is similar to some aspects of dance-movement therapy. And, second, the crucial component to facilitating better functioning is not self-reflection or awareness—it is social skills, which can be learned through repetition and imitation without much in the way of personal insight. These therapeutic interventions help people function better by helping them become interactive. Even low-functioning individuals with considerable mental or emotional challenges won't be institution-alized unless they are social problems. Similarly, one can go to see a Vodou mambo or priest for personal issues, but the cure or the therapy is inevitably social—one that will make the person tolerable to live with.

Dissociation is the main focus of this book and has been the central thread of my research since I returned to college as a 30-something undergraduate. It is a basic function of how our human brain works. Dissociation is a filtering, compartmentalizing, or apportioning of conscious awareness.[7] It is often used synonymously with the term "trance," but, as I point out in this book, trance is better considered the observable manifestation of dissociation. The general term dissociation is used in different ways in multiple disciplines because, after all, it means unassociated and can be applied to many things. My emphasis is on the psychological use of the term. Psychological dissociation is involved in everything from daydreaming, dissociative identity disorder, and alcohol intoxication to divine, transcendent revelation. I take my lead in this approach from psychological anthropologist Erika Bourguignon and her onetime student Felicitas Goodman. Bourguignon used the term dissociation to describe what happens in possession trance cultures such as Vodou, which she studied for many years. Bourguignon took a cross-cultural approach of exploring and explaining possession trance in a way that de-exoticized and translated it for Euroamerican readers.[8]

Goodman's story is interesting; she came to anthropology later in life, focused on the ethnology of glossolalia, and went on to found a New Age facility called the Cuyamungue Institute. Glossolalia is the ecstatic religious phenomenon where people speak in a non-human language attributed to God, aka "speaking in tongues." Her Institute is dedicated to rediscovering trance as a form of everyday relaxation through ritual postures. Goodman's early work, *Speaking in Tongues: A Cross-Cultural Study of Glossolalia*, published in 1972, was the first example of neuroanthropology (combination of neuroscience and anthropology) conducted among Apostolic Pentecostals, a path I later followed for my doctoral dissertation. Goodman worked in Indiana and Mexico, conducting ethnography of Pentecostals speaking in tongues and recording glossolalia to test the hypothesis that it has invariable linguistic features. She found, in brief, that while there are dialectic differences among groups, there are universal features of glossolalia that suggest it is neither a real language nor a faked non-language but something else entirely.[9]

Book Objectives

In this book, I outline how dissociation has been favored through processes of natural and socio-sexual selection to buffer the costs of consciousness. In Chapter 2, I address excesses of self-reflection or "thinking too much." Chapter 3 breaks down the models I have described above in more detail, discussing the primate experiments that suggest how and why self-awareness and theory of mind may have emerged in primates and the importance of dissociation in balancing these capacities in humans.

In Chapters 4 and 5, I explore the emergence of dissociation within what some call "ritual healing theory" and the "shamanic evolution of religion." These theories suggest that many of the characteristics commonly associated with organized religion and ethnomedical practices of modern foragers (or culturally relative, small-scale health-oriented practices) likely developed in concert with the evolution of our modern human species. For instance, anatomically modern *Homo sapiens* appear to have evolved from ancestors that could control and benefit from fire but may not have developed means to kindle fires anew until tens of thousands of years later. Fire is central in this context because of the role it may have played as a nexus for cognitive evolution and human self-domestication. Tending controlled fires would have required cooperation and communication, perhaps placing selective pressure on cognitive capabilities because of the marked advantage groups with controlled fire would have had over others. Furthermore, the relaxation effect we commonly associate with domestic fires (e.g., hearth or campfires) today may be more than cultural fascination. I discuss how fireside relaxation effects may have predisposed humans to dissociative relaxation via television and other media.

In Chapters 5 and 6, I examine the role of dissociation in altered states of consciousness and religious contexts. Following Goodman, I conducted my dissertation research among Apostolic Pentecostals in upstate New York. I became interested in dissociation as a central feature of religious ritual, which led me to explore whether speaking in tongues confers the same benefits as sitting around a fire (though, if you're keeping score, the order of my ideas and research don't quite follow this timeline). These disparate yet intersecting threads of inquiry exemplify the great diversity of dissociative cultural practices. As anthropologist Ulf Hannerz points out, diversity is the business of anthropology.[10] In Chapter 7, I explore some of that diversity, drawing on a wealth of ethnographic and psychological sources regarding Vodou, Santería, shamanism, dissociative identity disorder, hypnotherapy, meditation, and other culture-bound manifestations of dissociation. There are many ways for humans to find relief for the stress of conscious awareness. Such variation may facilitate a "dual inheritance" of biological predispositions for dissociation and adaptive sociocultural patterns of behavior that amplify those predispositions.

In Chapter 8, I untangle the terminology used to describe the psychological concept of dissociation, including "trance" and "deafferentation." The emergence of self-awareness in humans appears directly related to the human ability to be empathetic and to understand the possible minds of others. This may have benefited individual survival and reproduction in social groups. Ethnomusicologist Ruth Herbert makes a similar argument, pointing out that trance and hypnosis are often conflated. In her book *Everyday Music Listening*, Herbert argues that dissociation and trance get conflated in the literature because most sources do not distinguish psychological "state" from "process." The term "state" refers to temporary feelings that are dependent on circumstances, whereas "process" makes a semantic distinction, acknowledging that temporary feelings are not the result of flipping an on/off switch but involve active neurochemical changes. Herbert chooses to use the term "trancing" to evoke the process of dissociating. This avoids the linguistic problem of describing someone as "being in an altered state" or "being in a dissociative state," which suggests some global change rather than the fluctuating awareness that characterizes most everyday experience.[11] Herbert uses a definition of dissociation that is narrower than others, suggesting it is synonymous with "detachment" (inability to connect, in psychology) and is a type of trancing. In this sense, we can think of dissociation as synonymous with "zoning out."

I borrow the term "deafferentation" and its usage from neurophenomenologists Eugene d'Aquili and Andrew Newberg, who have found a variety of "mystical" states to be characterized by alternate stimulations and deafferentation in the brain.[12] Dissociation is a concept with numerous manifestations and different brain activity (or lack of activity) relevant to each state. Thus, there is no one neural correlate. Instead, there are what appear to be literal partitionings, shuntings, and preventions of certain neural pathways meeting other pathways. Afferent neural signals are those coming into a region (brain regions, in this case), whereas efferent are those leaving an area. Therefore, deafferentation refers to the prevention of incoming neural signals.

In Chapter 9, I discuss the mismatch of this evolutionary predisposition to limit consciousness and the addictive cultural innovations that facilitate dissociation, namely alcohol and drugs. Humans co-evolved with these substances, which may have exerted their own strong selective pressures because of the biochemical mechanisms inherent to them that facilitate dissociation. Some scholars posit, for instance, that human domestication of plants may have been motivated more by the desire for intoxicating substances than by the need for grain surpluses to provide for larger populations.

In Chapter 10, I outline another mismatch, that of self-deception. Self-deception is the ability to hold mutually exclusive ideas in mind without realizing it. This adaptation of consciousness may benefit people in mating and other social contexts. On the other hand, self-deception also enables people and polities to obscure underlying motives for actions that can be maladaptive. Evolutionary biologist Robert Trivers has long suggested, for instance, that the same quality which enables a person to project a confident self can be used by those in government to ignore signs of coming disaster created by their own overly confident decisions.[13]

In the last chapter, I suggest all of these qualities of dissociation, trance, and deafferentation are a model that can be nested in the theory of a behavioral immune system. Advocates of a behavioral immune system suggest that many cognitive predispositions are just as imperative as physiological responses in enabling humans to navigate environmental dangers.[14] For humans, the largest obstacle to success is other humans.

Notes

1 John McWhorter, *The Power of Babel* (New York: Holt, 2001).
2 N. Logothetis, "Vision: A Window into Consciousness," *Scientific American: Special Editions* 16, no. 3 (1999): 68–75.
3 Daniel J. Povinelli and J.G. Cant, "Arboreal Clambering and the Evolution of Self-Conception," *The Quarterly Review of Biology* 70, no. 4 (1995): 393–421.

4 Alan F. Dixson, *Primate Sexuality: Comparative Studies of the Prosimians, Monkeys, Apes, and Humans*, 2 ed. (Oxford: Oxford University Press, 2012).

5 Paul D. MacLean, *The Triune Brain in Evolution: Role in Paleocerebral Functions* (Springer Science & Business Media, 1990); Carl Sagan, *Dragons of Eden: Speculations on the Evolution of Human Intelligence* (Ballantine Books, 2012).

6 Allyson Barnacz et al., "Deception and Dating: Knowledge of Tactics May Improve Detection Accuracy," *Journal of Social, Evolutionary, and Cultural Psychology* 3, no. 1 (2009): 1–8.

7 Christopher D. Lynn, "Adaptive and Maladaptive Dissociation: An Epidemiological and Anthropological Comparison and Proposition for an Expanded Dissociation Model," *Anthropology of Consciousness* 16, no. 2 (2005): 16–50.

8 Erika Bourguignon, *Possession* (Prospect Heights, IL: Waveland Press, 1976); Felicitas D. Goodman, *How About Demons?: Possession and Exorcism in the Modern World* (Bloomington: Indiana University Press, 1988).

9 *Speaking in Tongues: A Cross-Cultural Study of Glossolalia* (Chicago: University of Chicago Press, 1972).

10 Ulf Hannerz, "Diversity Is Our Business," *American Anthropologist* 112, no. 4 (2010): 539–551.

11 Ruth Herbert, *Everyday Music Listening: Absorption, Dissociation and Trancing* (Ashgate Publishing Ltd., 2013); Kathryn A. Becker-Blease, Jennifer J. Freyd, and Katherine C. Pears, "Preschoolers' Memory for Threatening Information Depends on Trauma History and Attentional Context: Implications for the Development of Dissociation," *Journal of Trauma & Dissociation* 5, no. 1 (2004): 113–131.

12 Eugene G. d'Aquili and Andrew B. Newberg, "Religious and Mystical States: A Neuropsychological Model," *Zygon* 28, no. 2 (1993): 177–200.

13 Robert L. Trivers, *The Folly of Fools: The Logic of Deceit and Self-Deception in Human Life* (New York: Basic Books, 2011).

14 Mark Schaller and Lesley A. Duncan, "The Behavioral Immune System: Its Evolution and Social Psychological Implications," in *Evolution and the Social Mind*, eds. J.P. Forgas, Martie G. Haselton, and William von Hippel, 293–307 (New York: Psychology Press, 2007).

2

THINKING TOO MUCH

Is Thinking Too Much a Culture Syndrome?

In the 1960s, Canadian psychiatrist Raymond Prince was working in the then newly independent country of Nigeria in former British West Africa and noticed a unique constellation of symptoms among West African students of various ages, from secondary to university level. These students were literate but found themselves suddenly unable to read, grasp, or recall what they read or remember what they had just studied in ways that were atypical of the normal stress-induced or sleep-deprived forgetfulness common among students. He coined a name for this syndrome—"brain fag"—and his work went a long way toward reinforcing already entrenched ideas about European superiority and African inferiority. The diagnosis has since fallen out of fashion. Instead, clinicians and their clients prefer Western biomedical models of anxiety and depression.[1] While the term "brain fag" was used to describe a psychological disorder affecting West African intellectuals during a certain era, making it one of several "cultural syndromes" observed all over the world, cognitive disorders among educated classes—and those saddled with considerable social responsibilities as a consequence of their education—are extraordinarily common. Such disorders are related to having too many things on one's mind.

Anxiety and depression can result from repetitive or looping cognition, wherein a person gets stuck processing and reprocessing the same thoughts or worries over and over, resulting in the biological stress response. Nevertheless, anxiety and depression are not inevitable by-products of stress. For instance, despite considerable trauma associated with the Chinese invasion of Tibet in 1949 and political, economic, and penal privations Tibetans have suffered ever since, Tibetan refugees and exiles in Bhutan, Nepal, and India display less stress disorder than might be expected, as well as reticence to discuss their traumas. They indicate that their religion, Buddhism,

DOI: 10.4324/9781003034483-2

enables them to thrive regardless of widespread political violence and suffering. According to psychological anthropologist Sara Lewis, the Tibetan cultural practice of inculcating "spacious mind" prevents the looping cognition that could result in trauma. An 80-year-old Tibetan woman living in a moldy, one-room cement shelter in India, where she migrated with her family in the 1960s, describes the journey she endured to get there from Tibet as one that she was prepared for solely because she is Tibetan. An uneducated nomadic Yak herder, she and her three children fled from their village in the middle of the night when the local lama was "disappeared" and traveled through the Himalayas for four weeks by foot through Kathmandu to Dharamsala, India. One member of the party died, many developed frostbite, and all suffered nutritional deprivations. The Tibetan woman notes that she was prepared for these hardships by being brought up Buddhist; Buddhism helped her understand that suffering is part of life and that there are others who have it much worse.[2]

Suffering comes from the mind, according to Tibetans, not the external world. One 24-year-old Tibetan man Lewis interviewed who lost seven family members in a 2010 earthquake said it was their karma to die and his to live. "There were also many Chinese killed. The Chinese were frantic and wailing in the streets. Tibetans were much calmer. I don't think we were any less sad, but we accept death as a part of life. We also believe it does not help the situation to become very upset."[3] Despite the contention that this resilience is due to their religion, Lewis notes that many Tibetans are not particularly religious. Rather, they are raised to understand Buddhist principles as cultural values. The principles of Tibetan spacious mind derive from *lojong* ("mind training"), Buddhist techniques to deconstruct negative emotions and create mental space and flexibility. Tibetans are trained to stay mindful of the big picture and not get hung up on the details of current events or local problems. These techniques are so much a part of Tibetan daily life as to seem less like religious practice and more like what Americans would call "common sense." There will always be problems; such is life. Perseverating on problems, complaining about daily hassles, and giving in to strong emotions are toxic to the self and to those around you.[4]

While Tibetans are not immune to worry, the rates of trauma-related disorders among Tibetan refugees are far lower than expected based on data among refugees elsewhere. A criterion for posttraumatic stress disorder according to the *Diagnostic and Statistical Manual of Mental Disorders, Fifth Edition* (*DSM-5*, the most recent update to the American Psychiatric Association's taxonomic and diagnostic guide to mental disorders) is two or more symptoms (e.g., irritable behavior and angry outbursts, nightmares, hypervigilance, problems with concentration, etc.) that last at least a month or more following a trauma.[5] Tibetan nuns interviewed about being tortured evinced no such symptoms. Moreover, they knew of each other's shared experiences but had never been motivated to share their stories with each other, despite living together in the convent, until asked by foreign researchers. Tibetans seldom make use of psychological therapy; a Tibetan Department of Health clinic established for torture survivors reported providing services to only two individuals over the course of a year. A community organization started by ex-political prisoners to provide housing, language, vocational, and other material services sees far more clients, despite having its walls covered with photos of torture victims and corpses. The clients don't view the images as triggers that might retraumatize them but as proof of their mistreatment at the hands of the Chinese government. Multiple surveys of experiences of distress among Tibetans show that they rank symbolic actions such as the destruction of temples and forced religious renunciation as more upsetting than actions affecting their physical bodies such as imprisonment or torture.[6]

Tibetan attitudes seem strongly linked to Buddhist philosophy, as similar dispositions also appear among other Buddhists and those from regions with historically prominent Buddhist populations. Researchers who studied mental health impacts of an earthquake in Kobe, Japan, noted the cognitive dissonance between local cultural concepts of recovery and the western biomedical emphasis on testimonies and debriefing. Several scholars have noted local idioms of distress associated with "excessive thinking" that link it with psychosis and stigma. Many Tibetans identify "thinking too much" with *rlung* (pronounced "loong"), which translates as life-wind imbalance. Some symptoms of rlung map onto clinical depression and anxiety, such as insomnia, sadness, and body pain. Other symptoms are distinctive and largely somatic (affect the body more than the mind): dizziness, vertigo, syncope (sudden drop in blood pressure). Like depression and anxiety, rlung is believed to be a potential precursor for more serious symptoms, such as disorganized thinking and even psychosis in extreme cases. Strong negative emotions are seen to predispose Tibetans for rlung disorders, and, thus, Tibetans show concern for those they believe may be preoccupied with thinking. Indeed, Tibetans sometimes worry about those who enter monasteries to engage in Tibetan Buddhist philosophical studies, as such studying is known to lead to rlung.[7]

"Thinking too much" is a cultural syndrome, or collection of symptoms that are culturally recognized as a disease entity.[8] However, thinking too much resembles other cultural syndromes identified the world over. For instance, *nervios* is a condition of "altered nerves" that has been noted in Latin American countries and bears similarities to thinking too much. My University of Alabama colleague Kathryn Oths describes *debilidad* in the Peruvian Andes, which involves complaints of debility, exhaustion, and weakness, primarily of post-reproductive-age women.[9] Debilidad resembles *ataque de nervios* among Puerto Ricans and Costa Ricans, *nervos* in Brazil, *nevra* among Greek-Canadians, "nerves" in Kentucky, *susto* in Latin American, *sobreparto* and *macho wayra* in the southern Andes, "heart discomfort" in Iran, and *dysphorie* in France.[10] To these, psychological and medical anthropologist Bonnie Kaiser and colleagues add "thinking too much," described in over 20 cultures around the world, and in all cases linked to stress, anxiety, depression, or other nervous disorders.[11] In her work in Haiti, Kaiser finds sadness linked to thinking too much, particularly about money and hunger. These ruminations are not goal-oriented but instead involve preoccupation with one's plight. Having little to do leaves people too much time to sit and think, Haitian informants note, which also hampers them doing anything about their situations. "Once you stop playing soccer or cards, you start thinking again about the roots of your problems."[12]

Like Lewis' philosophy-studying Tibetan monks, US college students are often undermined by thinking too much, which may contribute more than what is generally acknowledged to clinical anxiety and depression. Multiple studies indicate that graduate students in particular have higher than average rates of anxiety and depression. My own research among anthropology graduate students and professionals attests to this—graduate students report significantly higher perceived stress and feelings of imbalance in their family-career interactions than professionals and more imbalance than even unemployed professionals.[13] It is not clear whether those predisposed to think too much are more likely to go to graduate school or if the inculcation of "critical thinking" that is part and parcel of higher education is the culprit. Likely, the high rates of student anxiety and depression are the results of interactions between a predisposition to be more reflective than the average person and the thinking too much that we university faculty literally train students to engage in.[14]

If thinking too much is such a common problem, why isn't it described more widely? Contrast the Tibetans in India described above with others in the same regions suffering the psychological and physical maladies commonly associated with stress-related disorders. Lesley Jo Weaver is a medical and psychological anthropologist who collaborates with Kaiser. Weaver works primarily with women in India coping with diabetes, women for whom "tension" is a chronic complaint. She lived with a woman named Shanti for several weeks while learning Hindi. Weaver describes Shanti as a cosmopolitan woman because she has a PhD in English literature and is one of the few divorcees Weaver has met in India. Shanti described herself to Weaver as strong and independent but also lonely, as she pined for her only son who had emigrated to the United States years before. Shanti kept her son's room exactly the way he had left it when he departed, and it represented the tension in her life between independence and loneliness and a refusal to let go of her own suffering. Shanti regularly slipped among bouts of raging, crying, brooding silence, and emotional happiness.[15]

Weaver notes that getting a grasp on a culture or cultural issue often revolves around a few words or concepts that are widely used and ambiguous without cultural or even situational context. "It might be hard to understand how Americans approach the world without a clear idea of the common term *stress*, and in particular the way middle-class American women self-consciously construct their identities around the idea of being stressed by competing life responsibilities. So, too, one might miss part of the picture of women's lives in India without a clear understand of *tension*."[16] For the women Weaver studies, the perseverative sadness is a chronic looping of thought for which they have little recourse, and it compounds physical health problems related to their diabetes. In fact, Indian women use the word "tension" to describe many of their daily struggles, even attributing conditions such as diabetes to it.[17]

Pivoting around Smartphones and Cigarettes

Like these Indian women or the Haitians Kaiser describes, many people around the world experience a relatively new but consistent stressor: the tension between being uncomfortably idle and compulsively engaged in social and political exchanges through cyberspace. This behavior pattern is emblematic of the human problem of chronic consciousness. Take, for instance, smartphones and the constant connection to information about cultural and societal conflicts they enable. Smartphones pique an evolved compulsion to play during what anthropologist Peter Stromberg calls the "extrastructural interludes" of life. Extrastructural interludes are periods outside structured segments of a day when we tend to get bored and seek stimulation. ·

While many of us chafe at an overstructured life, allowing us no time to relax, we often do not know what to do with ourselves during "down time." The priority people at all economic levels place on having televisions and now smartphones suggests something about the importance of being able to easily fill extrastructural time in ways that keep our minds occupied. Smartphones serve as a means of connecting socially and obtaining information, while also serving as what Stromberg and colleagues call a "pivot"—an object that facilitates the transformation into the space of play."[18] Furthermore, all the advertised features of smartphones—music, games, books, etc.—serve as pivots individually.

While the term "play" is typically reserved for what children do or for sports and games, play is a mammalian feature for learning social skills that is equally vital for adults. Play typically involves some rules, particularly in the case of certain games, and thus imposes structure on the interstitial space "to substitute for that which is missing."[19] Developmentally, play is how humans (and other mammals) build and test social contingencies or "scenario-build." Scenario-building is the term evolutionary biologist Richard Alexander coined to describe the human ability to think in the abstract. As he described, we don't merely "imagine;" we walk through contingencies in our minds to ascertain potential cause-effect chains of interactions in order to choose from among various courses of action. This utility of abstract thinking is the basic emergent capacity that many scholars attribute to consciousness or mind.[20] Playing is how people superficially and implicitly test scenarios and the boundaries of safety, both in social relationships and reality.[21]

In this sense, cigarette smoking is as much a pivot for play as smartphones are. People start off smoking even though they know it's bad to become addicted. According to medical anthropologist Mark Nichter, smoking is "socially engineered (advertised) to be an antidote for boredom."[22] Not only do cigarettes or other pivots give structure to ambiguous situations, they promote "social interaction, contributing to an atmosphere of egalitarian camaraderie."[23] Smoking provides an embodied feeling of belongingness. What is so interesting about choosing to smoke (or drink, or take drugs) to fill these spaces is that the activity comes with great risk. No one takes such risks without the promise of experiencing some pleasant physical or social sensation. "Play activity is closely patterned after something that already has a meaning in its own terms."[24] People play around things that have tremendous potential import, just like children pretend in their play to get married or have kids.

Defraying the Costs of "Analysis Paralysis"

These pivots are things we use to avoid "spinning," or repeatedly worrying about things we can't control. We use them as positive coping strategies to deal with "tension" or "stress" because, as we learned over the course of the 20th century, thinking too much invariably leads to anxiety and elevated blood pressure or heart palpitations—or vice versa if what we're worried about is our health. Stress-related disease displaced infectious disease as the leading cause of mortality in developed or industrial countries during the 20th century, leading to widespread interest in activities and behaviors that reduce stress.[25] Another way to understand this paradigm is to think of pivots as props or behaviors that facilitate dissociation in service of homeostasis. Homeostasis is equilibrium, and it's what our bodies return to after biological stress response or fight-or-flight. Just like the body, the mind cannot sustain too much of this fighting, fleeing, or anxiety, as indicated by extensive literature on the costs of chronic psychosocial stress. The mind needs a place to hide. Dissociation is necessary to limit the costs of self-awareness because these costs are stressful and cause problems. We can dissociate through an endless number of activities, some of them healthy (like, say, meditation) and others less so (cigarette smoking, for instance).

Dissociation is an important element of the allostatic stress response system. Allostasis is related to homeostasis or equilibrium, but is a state of adaptive change.[26] The concept of homeostasis suggests a single baseline state that stays the same throughout our lives. It is obvious, however, if one considers the changes we must go through as we grow, age, procreate, and modify our bodies through diet and exercise that there is no way our physiology and physique can maintain one state throughout life. The set points at which things like stress response are triggered also change as our bodies do. For instance, among experienced meditators, the threshold at which they become biologically stressed (e.g., lose their tempers) is higher than among a control group without such meditation expertise.[27]

The allostasis concept is generally applied to stress physiology—that is, the fight-or-flight responses that get activated when we are stressed and which are viewed as a departure from allostasis. But I suggest that behaviors through which humans purposefully moderate dissociation should be considered part of a *behavioral* allostatic system. I base this on the work of psychologist Mark Schaller, who developed the concept of the "behavioral immune system" to characterize systematic avoidance behavior.[28] The principle of the behavioral immune system is that avoidance behavior, stigmatization, and prejudice generally co-occur with varying degrees of disgust. Disgust, in turn, is associated with disease or things that may cause sickness or death and that therefore should be avoided.[29] Most neurobiologists indicate that vertebrates have two major activation systems—one that is appetitive (causing us to approach needed things to satiate a biological imperative) and the other avoidant, to help us withdraw from things that might kill us. While the appetitive/approach system is reinforced by rewarding experiences, the cost of failing to withdraw from danger exerts greater natural selection pressure (death) than failure to approach (hunger but not death).[30] Thus, erring to the side of caution, humans (and other vertebrates) tend toward high rates of false-negative behavior—avoiding strange or different others.[31]

Similarly, there are numerous cultural practices that, whether we are conscious of them or not, moderate the threshold of people's stress response. In discussing my research among Pentecostals, I have called speaking in tongues is a "behavioral homeostat." In stress physiology, homeostats are the individual mechanisms that facilitate maintenance of homeostasis, such as the hormones cortisol and epinephrine that increase blood pressure in stressful moments.[32] I call speaking in tongues a behavioral homeostat because it is a mechanism that moderates stress responses among Pentecostals (which I'll explain further in Chapter 5). When people are speaking in tongues, they are focused on God. In fact, according to practitioners, God has pushed them aside in their minds and is speaking *through* them. There literally is no room to think about anything else. If someone is thinking about bills, God won't come in. Worries are dissociated or partitioned from awareness at the moment one is speaking in tongues. Speaking in tongues is the mechanism that propels profound dissociation, to such an extent that practitioners feel they are no longer themselves.[33]

This system is allostatic in that practicing it leads to an increase in daily dissociation and reduction, to use Kaiser's phrase, of thinking too much. As one pastor I worked with said,

> We don't pray out loud because God can't hear our inner thoughts; we pray out loud so we don't start worrying about what we're gonna make for dinner, how our kids are doing in school, and so on. Praying out loud keeps us from cheating ourselves of our focus on God.

As with meditation and other cognitive techniques for stress reduction, prayer becomes easier with practice. When one has a problem and is able to put it in God's hands, it reduces the tendency to worry about things that one cannot resolve.

Anxiety and depression are not manifesting at epidemic levels, as research and news reports frequently assert. They are culturally endemic; they are by-products of how our human brains work and result from feelings and emotions considered culturally salient. In cultures that promote critical thinking and encourage us to listen to and consider diverse views, we are predisposed to anxiety and depression resulting from overwhelming and sometimes conflicting information. While I am not advocating for less education or a reduction in critical thinking, I am struck by the implication of Lewis' research that maybe we talk about problems too much. Repeating problems over and over shares anxiety, but it does little to alleviate it. Perhaps this is why, when I went through drug and alcohol recovery related to my own desire to turn off the repetitive thinking in my head, my sponsor told me to speak my problems once to him but not to share them at every meeting I went to. My recovery support system is there to help me, not to carry my anxieties alongside me.

In the next chapter, I examine indirectly whether these cultural psychiatric syndromes and disorders are unique to humans, exploring self-awareness and theory of mind in our closest primate relatives and ourselves.

Notes

1 Oyedeji A. Ayonrinde, Chiedu Obuaya, and Solomon Olusola Adeyemi, "Brain Fag Syndrome: A Culture-Bound Syndrome That May Be Approaching Extinction," *BJPsych Bulletin* 39, no. 4 (2015): 156–161; Raymond Prince, "The 'Brain Fag' Syndrome in Nigerian Students," *Journal of Mental Science* 106, no. 443 (1960): 559–570.
2 Sara E. Lewis, "Resilience, Agency, and Everyday Lojong in the Tibetan Diaspora," *Contemporary Buddhism* 19, no. 2 (2018): 342–361; "Trauma and the Making of Flexible Minds in the Tibetan Exile Community," *Ethos* 41, no. 3 (2013): 313–336.
3 "Trauma and the Making of Flexible Minds in the Tibetan Exile Community," 319.
4 "Trauma and the Making of Flexible Minds in the Tibetan Exile Community."
5 Association American Psychiatric, *Diagnostic and Statistical Manual of Mental Disorders (Dsm-5®)* (American Psychiatric Pub, 2013).
6 Lewis, "Resilience, Agency, and Everyday Lojong in the Tibetan Diaspora."; "Trauma and the Making of Flexible Minds in the Tibetan Exile Community."
7 "Trauma and the Making of Flexible Minds in the Tibetan Exile Community."; Sara E. Lewis, *Spacious Minds: Trauma and Resilience in Tibetan Buddhism* (Ithaca, NY: Cornell University Press, 2020).
8 Bonnie N. Kaiser and Lesley Jo Weaver, "Culture-Bound Syndromes, Idioms of Distress, and Cultural Concepts of Distress: New Directions for an Old Concept in Psychological Anthropology" *Transcultural Psychiatry* 56, no. 4 (2019): 589–598.
9 Kathryn S. Oths, "Debilidad: A Biocultural Assessment of an Embodied Andean Illness," *Medical Anthropology Quarterly* 13, no. 3 (1999): 286–315.
10 Meghan E. Keough, Kiara R. Timpano, and Norman B. Schmidt, "Ataques De Nervios: Culturally Bound and Distinct from Panic Attacks?" *Depression and Anxiety* 26, no. 1 (2009): 16–21; Charles C. Hughes, "Glossary of 'Culture-Bound' or Folk Psychiatric Syndromes," in *The Culture Bound Syndromes: Folk Illnesses of Psychiatric and Anthropological Interest*, eds. Ronald C. Simons and Charles C. Hughes, 469–505 (Dordrecht, Holland: D. Reidel, 1985); Ronald C. Simons, "Introduction to Culture-Bound Syndromes," http://www.psychiatrictimes.com/display/article/10168/54246; R.C. Simons and Charles C. Hughes, *The Culture-Bound Syndromes* (Dordrecht, Holland: D. Reidel, 1985).
11 Bonnie N. Kaiser et al., "'Thinking Too Much': A Systematic Review of a Common Idiom of Distress," *Social Science & Medicine* 147 (2015): 170–183.
12 Ibid.; Bonnie N. Kaiser et al., "Reflechi Twòp—Thinking Too Much: Description of a Cultural Syndrome in Haiti's Central Plateau," *Culture, Medicine, and Psychiatry* 38, no. 3 (2014): 458.
13 Christopher D. Lynn, Michaela E. Howells, and Max J. Stein, "Family and the Field: Expectations of a Field Based Research Career Affect Researcher Family Planning Decisions," (2018): e0203500.
14 Meghan Duffy, Carly Thanhouser, and Holly Derry, "A Lack of Evidence for Six Times More Anxiety and Depression in Us Graduate Students Than in the General Population," *Nature Biotechnology* (2019): 711–712; Teresa M. Evans et al., "Evidence for a Mental Health Crisis in Graduate Education," *Nature Biotechnology* 36, no. 3 (2018): 282–284; Loran F. Nordgren and Ap Dijksterhuis, "The Devil Is in the Deliberation: Thinking Too Much Reduces Preference Consistency," *Journal of Consumer Research* 36, no. 1 (2008): 39–46; Timothy D. Wilson and Jonathan W. Schooler, "Thinking Too Much: Introspection Can Reduce the Quality of Preferences and Decisions," *Journal of Personality and Social Psychology* 60, no. 2 (1991): 181–192; Katia Levecque

et al., "Work Organization and Mental Health Problems in PhD Students," *Research Policy* 46, no. 4 (2017): 868-879.

15 Lesley Jo Weaver, *Sugar and Tension: Diabetes and Gender in Modern India* (Rutgers University Press, 2018).

16 Ibid., 67.

17 Edward Evan Evans-Pritchard, *Social Anthropology* (London: Routledge, 2013); Weaver, *Sugar and Tension: Diabetes and Gender in Modern India* (New Brunswick, NJ: Rutgers University Press, 2018).

18 Peter Stromberg, Mark Nichter, and Mimi Nichter, "Taking Play Seriously: Low-Level Smoking among College Students," *Culture, Medicine and Psychiatry* 31, no. 1 (2007): 17; Kendall L. Walton, *Mimesis as Make-Believe: On the Foundations of the Representational Arts* (Harvard University Press, 1990); Lev Semenovich Vygotsky, *Mind in Society: The Development of Higher Psychological Processes* (Harvard University Press, 1980).

19 Stromberg, Nichter, and Nichter, "Taking Play Seriously: Low-Level Smoking among College Students," 1–24.

20 Richard D. Alexander, "Evolution of the Human Psyche," in *The Human Revolution: Behavioral and Biological Perspectives on the Origins of Modern Humans*, ed. Paul Mellars and Chris B. Stringer, 455–513 (Edinburgh: Edinburgh University Press, 1989).

21 Sergio Pellis and Vivien Pellis, *The Playful Brain: Venturing to the Limits of Neuroscience* (Oneworld Publications, 2013).

22 Stromberg, Nichter and Nichter, "Taking Play Seriously: Low-Level Smoking among College Students," 7.

23 Ibid., 9.

24 Erving Goffman, *Frame Analysis: An Essay on the Organization of Experience* (Harvard University Press, 1974), 40.

25 Robert M. Sapolsky, *Why Zebras Don't Get Ulcers, 2nd Edition: An Updated Guide to Stress, Stress Related Diseases, and Coping* (New York: W.H. Freeman, 1998).

26 David S. Goldstein and Bruce McEwen, "Allostasis, Homeostats, and the Nature of Stress," *Stress* 5, no. 1 (2002): 55–58.

27 Christopher R.K. MacLean et al., "Effects of the Transcendental Meditation Program on Adaptive Mechanisms: Changes in Hormone Levels and Responses to Stress after 4 Months of Practice," *Psychoneuroendocrinology* 22, no. 4 (1997): 277–295.

28 Mark Schaller and Lesley A. Duncan, "The Behavioral Immune System: Its Evolution and Social Psychological Implications," in *Evolution and the Social Mind*, eds. J.P. Forgas, Martie G. Haselton, and William von Hippel, 293–307 (New York: Psychology Press, 2007).

29 V. Curtis, M. de Barra, and R. Aunger, "Disgust as an Adaptive System for Disease Avoidance Behaviour," *Philosophical transactions of the Royal Society of London. Series B, Biological Sciences* 366, no. 1563 (2011): 389–401.

30 Antonio R. Damasio, *Descartes' Error: Emotion, Reason, and the Human Brain* (New York: Avon Books, 1994).

31 Mark Schaller, "The Behavioural Immune System and the Psychology of Human Sociality," *Philosophical Transactions of the Royal Society B: Biological Sciences* 366, no. 1583 (2011): 3418–3426; Mark Schaller and Damian R. Murray, "Infectious Disease and the Creation of Culture," in *Advances in Culture and Psychology Volume 1*, eds. Michele J. Gelfand, Chi-yue Chiu, and Ying-yi Hong, 99–151 (New York: Oxford University Press, 2011); Mark Schaller and Justin H. Park, "The Behavioral Immune System (and Why It Matters)," *Current Directions in Psychological Science* 20, no. 2 (2011): 99–103.

32 Goldstein and McEwen, "Allostasis, Homeostats, and the Nature of Stress."

33 Christopher D. Lynn, "Glossolalia Influences on Stress Response among Apostolic Pentecostals. Doctoral Dissertation" (PhD, University at Albany (SUNY), 2009).

3

THE MONKEY IN THE MIRROR

We're Definitely Bipedal Apes

Humans have an ability for self-awareness that may be at least indirectly related to our large-bodied mammalian ancestors' need for staying alive while locomoting through forest canopies. To put it another way, when we humans walk on our two legs, we don't worry about falling off the sidewalk, but when was the last time you tried climbing a tree? When the cable company shut my service off for no apparent reason on a Saturday morning before an Alabama football game, I found reason to climb one of those human-made "trees" that hold the cable connection junctions up out of our reach that (under normal circumstances) bring us endless hours of audiovisual distraction. The cable company wouldn't schedule a truck to come out to restore service until Monday. In Alabama, college football is religion, and I have become born again in crimson and white (the University of Alabama's team colors), so I decided to climb the utility pole in front of my house to try to reconnect my cable myself despite a fear of heights.[1] Those poles have rebar rungs sticking out the sides for climbing, so it was not like the stories my Samoan friends tell of shimmying up branchless coconut tree trunks using just the strength of their hands and knees. I was simply climbing up a vertical ladder. I made it to the top, but I soon realized the error of my judgment. Panicking like a kitten stuck in a tree, I clung to the top of the pole with every limb, finger, elbow, and toe, staring helplessly at the wires in front of me. Unable to even attempt a repair, I descended—arms and legs trembling from fear and exertion—like the obligate biped that I am.

The overweening self-reflection that I touched on in the last chapter appears unique to humans, and that may be due to its high cost, but where does it come from? How do we get from non-self-reflective ape ancestor to a species that has (so far) produced five editions of a manual for identifying and treating consciousness and mental disorders? My pathetic story—I failed in turning the cable back on and

DOI: 10.4324/9781003034483-3

had to follow the gamecast on my phone—hints at the answer, as does evolutionary psychologist Gordon Gallup Jr.'s recollection from his time as a graduate student at Tulane studying chimpanzee cognition. One day while shaving, Gallup thought, "I'm looking at myself in a mirror, knowing that the reflection I see is me, dragging a blade safely across my face to eliminate my beard stubble and foreground my glorious mustache." (Note: I may have taken liberties in paraphrasing this story, but as a former student of Gallup's and the owner of an elaborate mustache myself, I have fond recollections of my hours spent listening to him teach while he paced the room, pausing dramatically as he stroked his furry lip accoutrement.)

I was led to Gallup's lab by the research he conducted to test his mirror epiphany, which has become renowned as one of the most elegant experimental designs in consciousness research. Gallup was the first to conduct experimental tests of self-recognition in non-human primates by placing a painted dot out of the subject's line of sight except by a mirror on various anesthetized, mirror-habituated primates.[2] This protocol has been repeated by Gallup and others with all manner of primates, as well as in modified versions with numerous other species.[3] In the original experiment, chimpanzees and monkeys were habituated to a mirror by having one situated in their environment for ten days. Initially, monkeys and apes behaved antagonistically toward their reflections, as though encountering an unfamiliar monkey, but this behavior receded in the chimpanzees with repeated exposure to the mirror. After habituation, they were anesthetized and had marks placed on their heads that they could only see when looking in a mirror. Upon awakening, they had no access to a mirror and displayed no indication that they were aware of the marks. When presented with the mirror, chimpanzees touched the marks on their heads, not the mirror, and then examined their hands to see if it came off, suggesting they were aware of the marks as a change in self. The same was not true of the monkeys, which responded in a consistent agonistic way. They engaged in approach/withdrawal behavior with what appeared to be another monkey and then called it a draw, giving up in seeming boredom with the other monkey's rather bizarre and inappropriate behavior. Furthermore, a second group of chimpanzees was tested that had not been habituated to the mirror. These chimps behaved agonistically toward their reflection like the initial group had prior to habituation, and did not display mark-directed behavior.[4]

This set of experiments suggests that chimpanzees observe their reflection, become aware that it is a reflection of self, and thereafter use it to make self-oriented observations, whereas monkeys gain no such insight. Repeated studies of monkeys (platyrrhines and catarrhines, or what have historically been termed "New" and "Old World" primates, respectively) and chimpanzees confirm this. One pair of monkeys mirror-habituated over a 17-year period failed to ever recognize themselves in mirrors. Additionally, most other great apes, including orangutans and bonobos, display self-recognition using the mirror test.[5] Gallup infers not just self-recognition but self-*awareness* from this test, pointing out that (sighted) human individuals who lack or have impaired self-recognition, such as newborns and people on the autism and schizophrenia spectrums, have corresponding degrees of self-awareness. There are several criticisms of this inference, the most compelling of which comes from another former mentee of Gallup's, Daniel Povinelli.

But first, a word about gorillas. With three telling exceptions, gorillas don't fit the self-recognition pattern using mirrors. This is worth noting because, whereas chimpanzees and bonobos are more genetically related to humans through a common ancestor and a more recent divergence than are gorillas to human or even gorillas to chimpanzees and bonobos, the line that became orangutans diverged before gorillas. This phylogenetic discontinuity suggests a hominid ancestor of all great apes could recognize itself but that this ability was lost or greatly reduced in gorillas. The exceptions are three gorillas raised in captivity. Among them was the late Koko, taught by Penny Patterson to use American Sign Language. Koko received a modified mirror test; she was swabbed with a sham mark in four cases and a real mark in the fifth. She would touch the swabbed spot an average of 1.5 times in front of the mirror during each of the first four 10-minute sham cases but touched the spot 47 times when given the real mark. Other exceptions include Pogo and Bwana, zoo gorillas who were inadvertently marked with paint and reportedly used mirrors to observe and wipe the marks clean. These exceptions suggest that gorillas may have the capacity for self-recognition but that it is unrealized except under extraordinary circumstances, such as being raised by humans or in human-enriched environments.[6]

Climbing Trees for Science

Povinelli, whose work I introduced in Chapter 1, is a professional psychologist but also an amateur thespian, and calls on his theatrical skills in his profession to instruct and engage. I saw him transform a "lecture," without the use of notes or slides, into an improvisational demonstration of chimpanzee experiments using human audience members to enact chimp roles. Povinelli brought audience members down to the front and said, "You are a chimpanzee, and I have food; what do you do?"

Instinctively, the human actor knew a chimp would ask for the food: "Can I have some?" they asked.

"Chimps in the *Planet of the Apes* movies talk, but that's not real you know?" Povinelli quipped. The actor put their hand out. "That's better, but you're a chimp. You haven't been taught human manners or American social distance." The actor went closer, at which point Povinelli grasped the "chimp" by the wrist and pulled their hand right up into his own face. "This is how a chimp asks for food. They don't grab it out of your hand, but it's very clear what they're trying to communicate. Chimps and humans can understand each other's intent at a certain level, but the subtlety of human interactions that you learn implicitly is completely lost on them. Human social graces have zero relevance for chimpanzees in their normal environments, so why would we expect them to ever have such intuitions? This," states Povinelli, "is the basic problem with studies of chimpanzee theory of mind and self-awareness. Chimpanzees have no context for ever being able to understand a human mind, so testing for theory of mind using human protocols is a waste of time."

When I met him in 2009, Povinelli said he was done conducting primate cognition research.

> There's nothing more we can learn with the current technology that is as important as conservation. The bigger issue is how we will save these great ape species so they will still be around to study when the technology advances. All great apes will likely be extinct in the wild in our lifetimes, and captive populations lack genetic diversity and are as good as extinct already. I don't have enough hope in the political interest in saving them to believe we can change that. We almost had the State of Louisiana on board to support a large conservation facility for chimpanzees, but then Hurricane Katrina happened and then the recession, and that has been that. But it's more important to keep trying to protect them than doing more tests to determine if they can read my mind.

Povinelli had also studied under Gallup, albeit at a distance. Gallup was an outside member of Povinelli's dissertation committee at Yale and had helped him start his chimpanzee research facility when Povinelli was hired as an assistant professor at Louisiana-Lafayette. During a peak period of primate cognition studies in the 1990s, Povinelli's research was featured in popular documentaries like *Monkey in the Mirror*, which I still show to students nearly every semester.[7] Whereas Gallup suggests that self-recognition is evidence of self-awareness in chimpanzees and orangutans, Povinelli says that recognizing oneself isn't the same as being self-aware. In trying to resolve the problem of gorillas, Povinelli and anthropologist John Cant advance the "clambering hypothesis," to which my pole-climbing anecdote at the beginning of the chapter alludes. According to this hypothesis, self-recognition is not necessarily coupled with self-awareness but is probably a prerequisite.[8]

Why doesn't self-awareness just pop up all over the place? In addition to having the type of costly by-products outlined in the last chapter, such as analysis paralysis and self-doubt, self-recognition and self-awareness appear to be neurologically expensive. Even where ancestors may have been able to self-recognize, as with the probable ancestors of gorillas, expensive traits are unlikely to be retained if the benefits don't outweigh the costs. Self-recognition only appears in big-bodied apes that spend a lot of time climbing through the precarious three-dimensional space of trees; thus, self-awareness seems to be connected to enhanced proprioceptive awareness—awareness of one's own body in space. This type of self-awareness describes the slower clambering observed in orangutans that primatologists term "quadrumanous" locomotion—they use all four hands to carefully grab branches and spread out the distribution of their weight as they move. The selection pressures that favor proprioceptive awareness in other large-bodied non-human primates are probably relaxed in gorillas, suggest Povinelli and Cant. Gorillas locomote mostly on the ground because they have no natural predators despite the neural hardware to be self-recognizing if nurtured, as is the case with gorillas like Koko.[9]

The upshot is that self-awareness presupposes self-recognition but not necessarily the other way around.[10] I often demonstrate this in class by climbing up on the desks and walking from one to the other. I threaten to jump across, which is memorable for students, who are waiting for the old guy to fall down and bust his ass, but I never make the leap. I explain to them that I have enough proprioceptive awareness to recognize that I feel unstable as I'm doing it and that it could spell disaster. Sometimes I make the students get involved. We've gone outside and tried climbing trees, but very few students go farther than one branch up because they recognize their vulnerability, don't want to get dirty, or feel stupid—i.e., they are self-conscious about it. Then we go back inside and get up on the big long table in the conference room together. I ask them to imagine they are moving around on this table with each other as a family of monkeys might. They become very aware of their bodies in space and much less concerned about how cool they looked when they were posing in the lower branch of the tree.

Obviously, this is not evidence that self-awareness is not always coupled with self-recognition, but it suggests that there are circumstances where self-recognition is the key to survival and where self-awareness does little good.

Self-Awareness in Prehistory

We can see pieces of self-awareness in other species and imagine the component parts. Dogs are generally not considered as smart in human-like ways as our great ape relatives, but they are highly social and co-evolved with humans. Dogs are dependent on their ability to communicate with humans in their natural environments, whereas chimps, gorillas, and orangutans are not. Dogs therefore pass some of the human/dog ecosystem-relevant tests that chimps do not. For instance, while dogs don't pass the mirror test, they do follow human eye cues.[11] Human eyes are unique in showing more visible sclera (the whites of the eye) than other animals, making the direction of human gaze easy to discern from eyes alone.[12] Chimpanzees do not follow human eye cues. Chimps follow head movements only, but dogs will look where we look even if we only move our eyes to indicate direction of gaze.[13]

So perhaps we can take our dogs' perspectives to some extent and vice versa. My family's Siberian husky, Gallifrey, loves to wade in water but not to go so far that he has to swim. He also loves other dogs and will take off chasing them without thinking about the consequences (i.e., getting in trouble with dad). We were at a dog park in Bozeman, Montana, during vacation several years ago, a park that was so big it might as well have been a big open field. Gallifrey was safe from impulsively running into the road, but the dog park was too big for me to corner him if there were another dog he wanted to play with. Huskies are infamous for being stubborn and cantankerous, and for their skill as escape artists. They are highly social around humans and other dogs, but they score lower than many dogs on intelligence tests because such tests measure how well dogs respond to humans. Siberian huskies have the most recent introgression of wolf genes of any dogs whose genomes have been examined.[14] Perhaps, despite their co-evolution with us, intelligence tests for dogs are not species-relevant enough to capture what they are smart *at*. I had never seen Gallifrey actually swim before this outing, but there was another dog and dog-dad at the park. That dog was a retriever, and its owner was throwing a ball into a pond that the dog would swim out to retrieve. This was the first time Gallifrey had ever been off the leash when he saw dogs jumping into water. As soon as I let go of his leash, he bolted out after that dog to say hi and was halfway out into the pond before he apparently realized he was swimming and remembered that he didn't like to swim. So he turned around and bee-lined back. After that, he kept chasing the dog, but he would only wade a short distance into the water to try to get to it, all the while avoiding my grasp. So he obviously had some proprioceptive awareness of his body in space, and the pond was like the cable pole for me; he exhibited enough awareness of self to temper his response in both trying to catch the other dog without exceeding the limits of his comfort and in trying to avoid being caught by me. What is that if not some variety of intelligence or awareness?

Social psychologists Mark Leary and Nicole Buttermore outline a theory of self-awareness that breaks it into parts.[15] According to their model, human-variety self-awareness comprises five types of awareness about the world some of which appear in other species. These include information about ecological, interpersonal, extended, private, and conceptual self-knowledge. These separate domains, argue Leary and Buttermore, evolved somewhat independently to solve different environmental and social issues, which explains why some dimensions of self-awareness are evident in some animals and others in other animals. Only humans possess all five. "Ecological-self ability" is necessary for dealing with the immediate environment, whereas inter-personal-self ability is analogous except that it is used specifically for dealing with other members of one's species or, I would argue, species with which one has co-evolved, such as dogs. "Interpersonal-self ability" is like ecological-self ability in that neither requires reflection or special insight, which is how I would describe Gallifrey's behavior. Many pet owners would recognize this ability in our beloved dogs (and maybe, I grudgingly concede, in some of our cats). "Extended-self ability" enables organisms to reflect on themselves in the moment and over time. "Private-self ability" involves processing thoughts, feelings, and emotions not visible or apparent to others. "Conceptual-self ability" (what others refer to as symbolic self) involves the capacity to conceive in the abstract, including having concepts of self and a sense of identity.

Leary and Buttermore suggest that all protohominids or ancestors of great apes, as social mammals (like my husky), would have had ecological-self and interpersonal-self abilities. Furthermore, protohominids likely had at least a rudimentary sense of extended-self, as there is evidence that chimps and bonobos think about themselves over short terms, such as when they preemptively pick up a rock en route to a feeding site where they will use it to break open nuts. Limited private-self ability is also at least indirectly evident in some great apes, given the apes' abilities to deceive one another in relatively elaborate ways. There is no evidence of conceptual-self or symbolic ability in any of the great apes in natural conditions, though it could be argued that some such ability has been demonstrated in apes in captivity that have been taught to paint.[16]

Theory of Mind or Instinctive Social Intelligence

My sons are fraternal triplets who kept my wife and me busy when they were young. For instance, they stymied our efforts to use our lower kitchen cabinets for the intended purpose. When my boys were two-year-olds, they would continually go into the cabinets and pull out all the dishes. We feared they would get their hands on the cutlery at that age, disinfect each other's eyes, or look for fun with the dangerous chemicals under the sink. But the biggest problem was that all three kids could fit in one cabinet together and would crawl inside to play. They thought it funny to play smash-my-brother's-fingers-with-the-door-and-watch-him-cry. So I baby-proofed the kitchen, using pointed plastic latches that had to be pushed down to get a drawer or cabinet door open. But my son Lux was always a watcher. We had three high chairs lined up in the kitchen, and when they were sitting there with my wife during the day, his brothers Bailey and Jagger would play with the toys on their trays while Lux would watch their mother opening those cabinets. Within a few days, he was able to get them open himself, and games resumed. I feared they would slam the door into each other, poking each other in the eyes with the pointed childproofing latch. The cabinets had no external knobs I could lash together instead, so I installed handles and bought short bungee cords and bungeed the doors together. However, if bungeed too loose, Lux was soon able to open them. If too tight, my wife struggled to get them off. Finally, I found zip-tie-style childproofing, which worked until we moved to a new house.

There are a few widely used theory of mind test for humans. Autism researcher Simon Baron-Cohen developed the Sally-Anne "false belief" test with colleagues Alan Leslie and Uta Frith.[17] In this test, "Sally" hides an item in view of her friend "Anne," who then steps away and cannot see Sally's actions. Sally then moves the item to a different hiding place, whereupon Anne returns. When asking children below the age of approximately five years old where Anne will look for the item, they point to where the item currently is and don't seem to recognize that Anne holds a false belief. Around the age of five, children recognize that Anne will think the item is in its original hiding place because they have an accurate theory of how Anne's mind works. A few years later Baron-Cohen developed the "mind in the eyes" test to measure the extent to which people on the autism spectrum could accurately attribute mental states to others just from the eyes.[18]

It was clear my two- and then three-year-old children developed some intuitive awareness of the intention of others during that period of their lives and could observe a skill and then imitate it. Particularly Lux, who, though raised in the exact same environment as his brothers, seemed like he had a future as a master safecracker. It was around that time, while I was in graduate school, that I first learned about theory of mind and that human children did not pass the Sally-Anne false belief test until around the age of four or five. Since I had my own sample of three for developmental psychology research, I repeated this test among my boys. As a proud papa, I expected all three of them to pass—but, if not all three, then at least Lux. However, they all failed the test before they were five and all passed around the time they turned five. There were absolutely no differences among any of my kids or between them and other neurotypical children in the development of their ability to understand that others could hold false beliefs based on that test.

Whereas self-awareness is inferred from self-recognition in great apes and preverbal humans, scientific exploration of theory of mind is similarly hampered by the need to infer abilities from more limited capabilities that seem to lead to this higher-order function. The search for theory of mind in non-human primates has been fraught with difficulties, though the research is relatively new. By most accounts, it started with David Premack and Guy Woodruff's study investigating theory of mind in chimpanzees in a special journal issue dedicated to cognition and consciousness in non-humans in 1978, followed by primatologist Frans de Waal's *Chimpanzee Politics* in 1982, and two edited volumes by Richard Byrne and Andrew Whiten exploring "Machiavellian intelligence" in primates in the subsequent decade.[19] In many studies, purposeful deception by chimpanzees has been obvious and suggestive of theory of mind—i.e., it seems to indicate that chimps know enough about the minds of others that they see a need to be deceptive. Deception seems to indicate the ability to predict cause-effect behavior of others. However, other lines of theory of mind research have been inconclusive.

In the early 2000s, comparative psychologist Brian Hare and colleagues noted the problem of testing non-human primates in paradigms that were not ecologically relative or that used humans as social partners. To overcome this obstacle, they developed protocols that resembled naturalistic circumstances by involving intra-species hierarchical rank and food. For instance, they found that low-rank chimps would not go near food that they thought a higher-ranking individual had seen, even if the food was now hidden from the ranking individual. However, if it appeared the higher-ranking individual had not seen the food being hidden, the lower-ranking individual would surreptitiously approach and take the food, provided the other could not see them do it.[20]

As with self-awareness, these studies make clear the importance of considering theory of mind in component parts or via varying means of inference. Several early studies tested things that suggest non-verbal individuals and species possess some degree of theory of mind, such as gaze-following, perspective-taking, attention-reading, intention-reading, and attribution of others' false beliefs. In many early studies, the social partner for non-human subjects in these tests was a human, and results were predictably mixed. Gaze-following is an aspect of theory of mind that develops in human infants and is considered a critical aspect of social interaction. Gaze-following is notably absent in individuals with autism, a neurocognitive disorder characterized by theory of mind deficit. Chimpanzees can follow human gaze, but they don't infer mental states from this. However, the ability to infer a mental state improves when the social partner is a conspecific and, even more imperative, an actual friend. The most studied aspect of theory of mind in non-humans is perspective-taking, or imagining what another can or can't see from their point of view. This test of theory of mind is largely successful between conspecifics of different rank or close affiliates in relation to food. Subordinates seem especially keyed into what dominant members of a troupe see; however, no monkeys take into account the change from another's vantage. They can't imagine that the way an object is viewed from where another individual sits is different from where they themselves sit.[21]

Another aspect of theory of mind is level of attention. "Can they see what I see?" is one level. Higher-order theory of mind is "Are they paying attention to it/me?" Studies of attention focus on body orientation, eye gaze, and such. Most monkeys and apes cue into attention of conspecifics on some level, either gross body orientation or something more distinctive like eyes. Intention-reading studies examine the knowledge an individual has toward the purposeful versus accidental actions of another or the prosocial versus antisocial acts of another. Chimpanzees seem to recognize the difference in intention in both conspecific and human social partners. The false-belief paradigm represented by the Sally-Anne experiments with humans seems to represent the higher order of theory of mind of which only humans are capable.

Nonetheless, newer experimental designs that are more ecologically relevant make it apparent that apes and monkeys possess both self-recognition and theory of mind to some degree. Philosopher Stephen Butterfill and psychologist Ian Apperly suggest that many social interactions involving theory of mind are quick and impressionistic, not requiring higher-order processing. They call this "minimal theory of mind." More elaborate social interactions, such as what humans exhibit, require "full-blown theory of mind cognition."[22] Minimal theory of mind may be an automatic sub-mentalizing form that is domain-specific and does not involve actually thinking about others' mental states or reasoning about actions.[23]

Recent paleoanthropology finds of new species named *Homo naledi*, *Homo denisovan*, *Homo floresiensis*, and *Homo luzonensis* reinforce that cognitive sophistication in our genus has not been as unique as previously thought, and thus not necessarily what led to the ascendant success of *Homo sapiens* alone above all others.[24] Dating on *Homo naledi*, for instance, suggests it was well within the Anthropocene (the current geological age dominated by humans) but with a brain the size of an orange. This is amazing because the *Homo naledi* remains were found in a place and in such a way that suggests the bodies were purposefully placed there by conspecifics who went to a great deal of trouble and would have needed to communicate to coordinate their efforts. The time frame for *Homo naledi* is consistent for when scholars think symbolic thought was developing, but the allometry of the brain (relative to body size) is all wrong for what was assumed necessary to have the smarts required.[25]

Neural networking and integration of brain areas is more predictive of intelligence than is absolute size, but there is a physics problem in that a certain amount of cerebral real estate was thought necessary to accommodate the integration for symbolic thought.[26] Psychologists Constantine Sedikides and John Skowronski further suggest that *Homo erectus* was developing symbolic thought because of the apparent increase in brain size during this period and because it seems that cooperative hunting had become more essential.[27] Merlin Donald suggests that *Homo erectus* could consciously mimic each other in ways that would have been communicative but not linguistic and that entailed private-self ability. *Homo naledi* throws a wrench in the social brain hypothesis, which suggests that increasing social sophistication drives the enlargement of the brain.

Yet, it is not at all clear that any of this social behavior needs to be conscious, whether a species has linguistic capabilities or not. A somewhat outdated theory that is nonetheless evocative here is psychologist Julian Jaynes' concept of a "bicameral mind." The premise is that self-awareness is a recent invention of the Greeks. Jaynes suggested the experience of having a new idea is something rare enough that, even today, many people attribute them to "divine inspiration." New ideas may have been even rarer in antiquity, when human group sizes were small and exposure to things and people that were different would have been significantly reduced. A new idea would have been as ineffable as a natural disaster and subject to supernatural explanation. As his evidence, Jaynes noted the shift in mentation between Homer's epics. In *The Illiad*, most human activity is attributed to intervention by the Gods, whereas Odysseus displays significantly more agency in his decision making in *The Odyssey*. Jaynes attributes this shift to a decline in the societal importance of Gods during the Greek period, which has continued ever since.[28]

Humans still often attribute their own thinking to outside sources. Pentecostals refer to abilities to play music or sing in the Church as "gifts of the Spirit." Testifying about one's spiritual experiences is "God working through" a person. A person can be possessed by demons as well, leading them to act out and misbehave. In one example I'll return to in Chapters 5 and 6, a person's behavior was attributed to a combination of demonic possession and "getting in her own way." Carlos David Londoño Sulkin writes of the Amazonian belief that certain animals are characterized by certain tendencies. When humans display those tendencies, it's because they are possessed by those animals.[29]

Thus, it's highly likely that awareness and consciousness are not fully integrated things and that, in fact, we humans are hardly aware or conscious of why we do the things we do much of the time, although we may be able to scrounge up an explanation if pressed. In the next chapter, I explore why humans may have started cooperating, focusing on the use of fire as a key element in both the environmental and social pressures leading to human awareness of others' intentions.

Notes

1 Eric Bain-Selbo, "From Lost Cause to Third-and-Long: College Football and the Civil Religion of the South," *Journal of Southern Religion* 11 (2009), http://jsr.fsu.edu/Volume11/Selbo.htm.
2 Gordon G. Gallup, Jr., "Mirror-Image Stimulation," *Psychological Bulletin* 70, no. 6 (1968): 782–793.
3 Dawson Clary et al., "Mirror-Mediated Responses of California Scrub Jays (Aphelocoma Californica) During a Caching Task and the Mark Test," *Ethology* 126, no. 2 (2020): 140–152.
4 Gordon G. Gallup, Jr., "Chimpanzees: Self-Recognition," *Science* 167, no. 914 (1970): 86–87; "Mirror-Image Stimulation."; Gordon G. Gallup, Jr., J. Anderson, and Daniel Shillito, "The Mirror Test," in *The Cognitive Animal: Empirical and Theoretical*

Perspectives on Animal Cognition, ed. Marc Bekoff, Collin Allen, and Gordon G. Burkhardt, 325–334 (Cambridge: MIT Press, 2002).

5   M.D. Hauser et al., "Self-Recognition in Primates: Phylogeny and the Salience of Species-Typical Features," *Proceedings of the National Academy of Sciences of the United States of America* 92, no. 23 (1995): 10811–10814.

6   Sue Taylor Parker, "Incipient Mirror Self-Recognition in Zoo Gorillas and Chimpanzees," in *Self-Awareness in Animals and Humans*, eds. Sue Taylor Parker, Robert W. Mitchell, and Maria L. Boccia, 301–307 (Cambridge: Cambridge University Press, 1994); D.H. Ledbetter and J. Basen, "Failure to Demonstrate Self-Recognition in Gorillas," *American Journal of Primatology* 2, no. 3 (1982): 307–310; D.J. Shillito, Gordon G. Gallup, Jr., and B.B. Beck, "Factors Affecting Mirror Behaviour in Western Lowland Gorillas, Gorilla Gorilla," *Animal Behaviour* 57, no. 5 (1999): 999–1004; Gordon G. Gallup, Jr., L.B. Wallnau, and S.D. Suarez, "Failure to Find Self-Recognition in Mother-Infant and Infant-Infant Rhesus Monkey Pairs," *Folia primatologica; International Journal of Primatology* 33, no. 3 (1980): 210–219.

7   Karen; Posner Bass, Mara; Aldrich-Blake, Pelham, "Monkey in the Mirror," *Nature* 517, (1995): 246.

8   Daniel J. Povinelli and J.G. Cant, "Arboreal Clambering and the Evolution of Self-Conception," *The Quarterly Review of Biology* 70, no. 0033–5770 (1995): 4.

9   Ibid.

10 J.R. Anderson and Gordon G. Gallup, Jr., "Self-Recognition in Nonhuman Primates: Past and Future Challenges," in *Animal Models in Human Emotion and Cognition*, eds. Marc Haug and Richard E. Whalen (Washington, DC: American Psychological Association, 1999).

11 Brian Hare and Michael Tomasello, "Domestic Dogs (Canis Familiaris) Use Human and Conspecific Social Cues to Locate Hidden Food," *Journal of Comparative Psychology* 113, no. 2 (1999): 173–177; Ernő Téglás et al., "Dogs' Gaze Following Is Tuned to Human Communicative Signals," *Current Biology* 22, no. 3 (2012): 209–212.

12 Hiromi Kobayashi and Shiro Kohshima, "Unique Morphology of the Human Eye," *Nature* 387, no. 6635 (1997): 767–768.

13 Brian Hare and Michael Tomasello, "Human-Like Social Skills in Dogs?" *Trends in Cognitive Sciences* 9, no. 9 (2005): 439–444.

14 Xuan Wang et al., "Canine Transmissible Venereal Tumor Genome Reveals Ancient Introgression from Coyotes to Pre-Contact Dogs in North America," *Cell Research* 29, no. 7 (2019): 592–595.

15 Mark R. Leary and Nicole R. Buttermore, "The Evolution of the Human Self: Tracing the Natural History of Self-Awareness," *Journal for the Theory of Social Behaviour* 33 (2003): 365–404.

16 Ibid.

17 Simon Baron-Cohen, Alan M. Leslie, and Uta Frith, "Does the Autistic Child Have a "Theory of Mind"?" *Cognition* 21, no. 1 (1985): 37–46.

18 Simon Baron-Cohen et al., "The 'Reading the Mind in the Eyes' Test Revised Version: A Study with Normal Adults, and Adults with Asperger Syndrome or High-Functioning Autism," *The Journal of Child Psychology and Psychiatry and Allied Disciplines* 42, no. 2 (2001): 241–251.

19 David Premack and Guy Woodruff, "Does the Chimpanzee Have a Theory of Mind?" *Behavioral and Brain Sciences* 1, no. 4 (1978): 187–192; Frans B.M. de Waal, *Chimpanzee Politics: Power and Sex among Apes*, vol. Revised (John Hopkins University Press, 1998); Richard W. Byrne and Andrew Whiten, *Machiavellian Intelligence: Social Expertise and the Evolution of Intellect in Monkeys, Apes and Humans* (Clarendon Press, 1988); "Machiavellian Intelligence," in *Machiavellian Intelligence Ii: Extensions and Evaluations*, ed. Andrew Whiten and Richard W. Byrne (Cambridge: Cambridge University Press, 1997).

20 Brian Hare et al., "Chimpanzees Know What Conspecifics Do and Do Not See," *Animal Behaviour* 59, no. 4 (2000): 771–785; Michael Tomasello, Josep Call, and Brian

Hare, "Chimpanzees Understand Psychological States—The Question Is Which Ones and to What Extent," *Trends in Cognitive Sciences* 7, no. 4 (2003): 153–156.

21 Hélène Meunier, "Do Monkeys Have a Theory of Mind? How to Answer the Question?" *Neuroscience & Biobehavioral Reviews* 82 (2017): 110–123.

22 Ian A. Apperly and Stephen A. Butterfill, "Do Humans Have Two Systems to Track Beliefs and Belief-Like States?" *Psychological Review* 116, no. 4 (2009): 953–970; Stephen A. Butterfill and Ian A. Apperly, "How to Construct a Minimal Theory of Mind," *Mind & Language* 28, no. 5 (2013): 606–637.

23 Cecilia Heyes, "Apes Submentalise," *Trends in Cognitive Sciences* 21, no. 1 (2017): 1–2.

24 Lee R. Berger and John David Hawks, *Almost Human: The Astonishing Tale of Homo Naledi and the Discovery That Changed Our Human Story* (National Geographic Books, 2017); Lizzie Wade, *New Species of Ancient Human Unearthed* (American Association for the Advancement of Science, 2019).

25 Berger and Hawks, *Almost Human: The Astonishing Tale of Homo Naledi and the Discovery That Changed Our Human Story.*

26 Harry J. Jerison, *Evolution of the Brain and Intelligence* (Academic Press, 1974).

27 Constantine Sedikides, John J. Skowronski, and Robin I.M. Dunbar, "When and Why Did the Human Self Evolve?" in *Evolution and Social Psychology*, ed. Mark Schaller, Jeffry A. Simpson, and Douglas T. Kenrick, *Frontiers of Social Psychology* (Philadelphia, PA: Psychology Press, 2006).

28 Julian Jaynes, *The Origin of Consciousness in the Breakdown of the Bicameral Mind* (Houghton Mifflin Harcourt, 2000).

29 C.D. Londoño Sulkin, "Paths of Speech: Symbols, Sociality and Subjectivity among the Muinane of the Colombian Amazon," *Ethnologies* 25, no. 2 (2003): 173–194.

4

COGNITIVE EVOLUTION AND FIRESIDE RELAXATION

Bickering by the Fire: An American Pastime

Human evolution around domestic fires, such as those in a hearth or campfire, has likely played a significant role in the amplification of dissociative capacities in humans. We use fires as pivots or fulcrums around which we gather, but fires have also been a centrifugal force in human evolution. When my triplet boys were two years old, my wife and I took them camping for the first time, along with my in-laws. We went to a little lake in upstate New York with a campground, my in-laws at one campsite and my crew at another adjacent to them. Meanwhile, across the campground, friends of ours with one child approximately the same age as our three were also camping that weekend. It was a two-night outing, and there were thunderstorms both nights, though the days were relatively clear. My wife and I started bickering while setting up the tent, and our tension worsened through the first night of rain. The tent leaked at the edges, and everyone whined about the dampness all night. The boys have always squabbled, since they were old enough to roll over and steal binkies from each other's mouths. We rose the next morning in foul moods, angry about everything. My wife thought it wasn't worth staying the whole weekend in the rain, and I was angry that she was ready to pack it in. She pointed to the boys' unhappiness as evidence that no one was having fun. I said we needed to tough it out and not quit on what is an essential part of "the camping experience." Our friends had an angrier night than we did, and my mother-in-law was also ready to go home. However, the weather cleared, and our moods lightened a bit. After a few daytime activities, we set ourselves the challenge of starting a fire using wood kept dry in the car.

As the wood crackled and we moved close to warm ourselves, the aggravation dissipated. We roasted hot dogs, made s'mores, and sat chatting as we gazed into the flames. The kids threw sticks into the campfire to watch them burn as I adjusted

DOI: 10.4324/9781003034483-4

logs and looked for excuses to add more wood. Our friends across the campground reported a similar experience. They relaxed by their fire, and their child sat by it until he nodded off to sleep. Nine months later, they had their second child!

Camping is one of those things White middle-class Americans on TV seem to do. Evolutionary psychologist Daniel Fessler has suggested that this cultural practice and media depictions of it as a normal activity biases Americans to think that everyone loves fire. Based on a preliminary survey, he initially suggested that fire is most fascinating for cultures wherein there is only limited exposure during childhood.[1] Cultures where fire is central to daily activities would find it more mundane. This "fire exposure hypothesis" was tested by Fessler's student Damian Murray (now assistant professor at Tulane University) in North American samples with different degrees of fire exposure during childhood, but he found no differences. Fire was equally enthralling to adults from both groups regardless of previous exposure.[2] Anthropologist Polly Wiessner has explored fire use among the !Kung of the Kalahari and in Papua New Guinea and found that interest in fire as a social nexus depends on context. During the day, fires are largely utilitarian things used for cooking and such. But at night, when daily work is finished, circadian hormone rhythms enable relaxation, and natural light fades, fires become a central focus for communities. Fires are where people gather to tell stories and the flickering light and crackling sounds give people an audiovisual pivot around which to focus attention.[3]

When I was in graduate school, I read a paper by sociologist James McClenon that suggested cultural healing practices probably arose in these contexts.[4] Since *Homo erectus* could control but not start fires, and fires are so relaxing, McClenon proposes, those individuals who were most receptive to fire's calming influence were probably more approachable. This opportunity to relax, McClenon suggests, would have been advantageous to health, and those even-keeled individuals who were able to use the presence of fire to calm their temperaments would have been attractive social partners to have as friends or mates. I remember thinking that this theory sounded like a "just-so story" (so-called based on the Rudyard Kipling stories about things that serve different purposes now than those they evolved or were invented for?). Why might *Homo erectus* have been predisposed to find fires relaxing, I wondered. Does everyone really find fires relaxing? Or, as Fessler suggests, do we just have a cultural preoccupation with them? And if campfires do stimulate a predisposition for dissociative relaxation, where does that predisposition come from?

Hypnotizing Chickens

Dissociation is not a specialized function that evolved in humans to combat consciousness. It is likely a basic function of psyche that derives from the fight-flight-or-freeze stress response. Hypnosis provides some insight into this. For instance, you can hypnotize practically any living thing. Hypnosis is a form of dissociation that includes both the partitioning of awareness, which is the focus of this book, and suggestibility, which is what makes it interesting to the general public. Gordon Gallup, Jr. whose mirror test for self-recognition I wrote about in Chapter 3, is also noteworthy because he used to hypnotize chickens for science. Chicken hypnosis is referred to as tonic immobility, a capacity for becoming seemingly catatonic under stressful conditions that has been observed in numerous species. Gallup induced tonic immobility in chickens by manually restraining an animal, holding its head at the ground, and drawing a line starting at the beaks and extending outward. The chickens then remained immobilized for a period of from 15 seconds to up to 30 minutes. This capacity in fowl has long been recognized, though the first known mention of animal hypnotism in print dates at least to a printing of the Old Testament. Gallup and others suggest that tonic immobility is part of fear response, as a defense mechanism that feigns death, akin to playing possum.[5]

Gallup and colleagues conducted multiple studies of tonic immobility in chickens to explore evolutionary hypotheses, and he concludes that the variability in duration times observed is in part due to genetic factors. In one controlled study, they retained chickens whose durations of tonic immobility were longest and shortest. These chickens were randomly mated within groups, and the next generation was assessed. The durations of tonic immobility in the offspring generations remained similar to their respective parent groups, suggesting that 75–90% of within-group variance in tonic immobility is genetically determined. Note, duration is distinct from susceptibility to tonic immobility, and some chickens that are highly susceptible may exhibit it for relatively short durations. Since birds are direct descendants of dinosaurs, the fact that we see this capacity in chickens and other animals suggests deep phylogenetic roots. Tonic immobility has been observed to varying degrees in insects, crustaceans, fish, amphibia, reptiles, birds, rats, rabbits, and primates.[6]

If tonic immobility is a heritable but variable trait, then humans should show similar evidence. There is a growing body of research suggesting a genetic basis for at least some aspects of hypnotizability in humans. Israeli psychiatrist Pesach Lichtenberg and colleagues have conducted a number of studies over the past few decades testing the "dopaminergic mechanism of hypnosis" hypothesis. Dopamine is an appetitive or "reward" hormone that increases positive feedback of activities associated with it, like eating or having sex, as basic examples. Earlier studies showed higher levels of a dopamine metabolite called homovanillic acid in the cerebrospinal fluid of highly hypnotizable people. Lichtenberg and colleagues suggest that variation in the polymorphic gene for catechol-O-methyl transferase (COMT) might be a factor for some degree of heritability in this dopaminergic activity. While they acknowledge that the hypnotizability concept includes biological, cognitive, and social elements, COMT influences the metabolism or removal of dopamine in some brain pathways. The genotype that results in less COMT production is associated with higher dopamine activity and better "sensorimotor gating," or the regulation of sensory transmitted to motor output systems.[7] Such gating appears to regulate some of the dissociation observed between sensory and motor systems in hypnosis, and, we can speculate, may also play a role in screening conscious awareness of sensory and motor activities.

Hypnotic abilities seem therefore to have at least some genetic basis, and there is good reason to further speculate that this ability to slip into hypnotic states has become more complex in humans, who tap into it for other purposes than just to escape or deal with fearful circumstances, such as to focus the mind and relax while sitting around fires. Several lines of circumstantial evidence suggest that domestic fires may have played a significant role in human cognitive evolution. The best such evidence for the antiquity of human control of fire comes from "phantom hearths" or evidence of repeated purposeful fire without remnants of the hearth. The best known site of such phantom hearths is Gesher Benot Ya'aqov in modern day Israel, dated to around 790,000 years ago.[8] McClenon speculates about this period of *Homo erectus* dispersal into the more temperate and colder northern areas of what are today Europe and Asia in developing his "ritual healing hypothesis."[9] McClenon suggests that fireside behavior would have been marked with several features evident in shamanic and possession rituals noted historically and projected back in time to attempt to explain things like the evolution of religion. For instance, researchers suggest that human ancestors, beginning perhaps as early as *Homo erectus* 800,000 or more years ago, gathered together to behave in routinized ways (that we tend to call "ritual," though sacredness is often inferred when we use that term) in efforts to control soothe person and group anxieties. Such behaviors extend from such typical social mammal activities like grooming, eating, and snuggling to repetitive movements and noisemaking. Repetitive self-soothing behavior, called "stimming" in clinical human contexts but common in all humans (e.g., tapping on a table, knuckle-cracking, mustache-chewing), is common in mammals, and anthropologist Michael Winkelman has suggested that noisemaking behaviors, such as using sticks to bang on trees observed among groups of chimpanzees, may be similar to forms of group "ritual" self-soothing behavior, such as humans sitting around fires to commune and self-soothe. Such rituals take place at night, when biorhythms are relaxed, and around domestic fires that, combined with low surrounding light, increase chances of perceptual distortions. People are more relaxed but also more suggestible, with greater potential to be frightened by a ghost story, fall under the spell of rousing tales of the ancestors, or bond via the unifying cadences of sing-alongs.[10]

The firelight is a visual fulcrum, making other shapes difficult to discern. It is hypnotic in its flickering and crackling intensity, and narcotic in its warmth. The food, drink, music, and dance of the evening combine with these elements to serve as triggers for dissociative trance states—a scenario familiar and compelling to modern sensibilities. McClenon believes humans over the millennia were drawn to these properties of fire and seized on its beneficial capacity to heal the days' ills.[11]

This imagined context resembles what anthropologist Melvin Konner observed in his apprenticeship with the Kalahari !Kung in the 1970s, which he refers to as "transcendental medication."[12] Konner's play on words refers to Transcendental Meditation, which was at the height of its popularity at the time of his coinage, due in part to successful initiation of George Harrison and The Beatles by the Maharishi Mahesh Yogi. Through the ensuing decades, the Maharishi School of Management in Fairfield, Iowa, founded by the Maharishi, applied this system of meditation, derived from the more ritualized Ayurvedic practice for a largely secular Western audience, to advance healthy lifestyles and reduce stress-related disease. A series of studies have demonstrated the efficacy of Transcendental Meditation in reducing blood pressure and positively impacting cardiovascular disease, among other non-communicable, stress-related maladies.[13] Similar results have been associated with mindfulness meditation as well. In the 1970s, medical doctor Herbert Benson distilled the stress-reducing essence of Transcendental Meditation as the "relaxation response." His book of the same name gave this secret and the training to practice it away for the cost of the paperback, which was several thousand dollars less expensive than Transcendental Meditation training.[14] Benson and his colleagues have also conducted numerous studies demonstrating the efficacy of this approach to stress reduction and outlining the mechanisms of relaxation response.[15]

Relaxation response is the physiological counterpart to stress response. These interrelated sides of the same system ideally operate in dynamic balance or allostasis. As I touched on in earlier chapters, allostasis is distinguished from homeostasis, which means maintaining balance, by the emphasis on environmental or lifecycle dynamics.[16] In experimental studies using the technique of Relaxation Response (capitalized when specifically referring to their published protocol) designed by Benson and derived from Transcendental Meditation, his team explored the physiological mechanisms of allostasis. For instance, cortisol, epinephrine, and norepinephrine are the key hormones associated with the induction of stress response and partly responsible for "allostatic load," or the unhealthy accumulation of negative consequences associated with chronic stress. Benson's colleagues and medical doctors Tobias Esch, Gregory Fricchione, and George Stefano, researchers at Massachusetts General Hospital's Mind/Body Medical Institute, indicate that melatonin and nitric oxide are lesser known but also central to stress response.

Relaxation response is associated with most if not all of the same physiological pathways as stress response. For instance, sensitivity to norepinephrine can be reduced by regular use of relaxation response technique, meaning the stress response system has a higher threshold for activation caused by norepinephrine production. This change in set-points appears to occur through the production of nitric oxide in multiple forms (e.g., constitutive, as part of regular physiological functioning, or inducible, as occurs in overwhelming and chronic stress situations) that can interact in beneficial or detrimental ways. Relaxation techniques of various kinds (including Relaxation Response, as well as meditation, tai chi, yoga, progressive muscle relaxation, autogenic training, and biofeedback) are effective in lowering systolic and diastolic blood pressure. This appears to occur through the vasodilation function of constitutive nitric oxide, increases of which are associated with these relaxation techniques.[17]

The genetics and selection regimes of nitric oxide, nitric oxide synthase variants, and other candidate mechanisms in the stress/relaxation response complex are not well studied. Nevertheless, it is possible that dissociative or relaxation capacities were amplified through evolutionary processes in the same way that features of tonic immobility were amplified through selective chicken breeding. McClenon posits that *Homo erectus* would have found fires at night relaxing for the same reason people today do and that those who were more approachable under such circumstances would have benefited socially compared to those less approachable. People are more social sitting around fires, he suggests. McClenon even posits a selection favoring those more gregarious by fireside, as they would have been preferred leaders, less volatile, more trustworthy.[18] While it is impossible to test this scenario in antiquity, it resembles the dynamic outlined by primatologist Frans de Waal in his book *Chimpanzee Politics* and other writings. Individuals better able to get along with others are often more successful at obtaining power through implicit coalition formation than those who rely on physical force without the backing of friends.[19] This scenario has been termed "self-domestication" by cognitive scientists Brian Hare and Richard Wrangham, among others, and is supported by a wealth of evidence, as outlined in Hare and partner Vanessa Wood's book *Survival of the Friendliest: Understanding Our Origins and Rediscovering Our Common Humanity*.[20]

This self-domestication through friendliness theory builds on Wrangham's "cooking hypothesis." Human brain expansion, tooth size reduction, and gut changes occurred at a rate that would be odd were cooking meat not a cornerstone of human evolution.[21] Yet how did humans accomplish this without coordination? Maintaining fire required as much cooperation as cooking food or hunting, if not more. According to archaeologist John Gowlett, there is no evidence that humans could kindle a fire before 40,000 years ago.[22] The archaeological record is difficult to interpret in this regard, as it's not possible to tell if the absence of evidence is due to the limited or non-existence of the behavior or eradication of traces by glaciation and other climatic forces. Human-controlled fire would most likely have existed in cold regions where glaciers have wiped away evidence and therefore where traces of fire manipulation are likely to have been erased. The locations where evidence for early fire has been found are far-flung and without clear patterning. However, as it stands, there is roughly a 750,000-year span between the emergence of humans' ability to control and to start fire that may have been sufficient time to provide the selective pressure for the elaboration of human cooperation, development of language, and expansion of the human brain. And thus, while not the only influence, these evening fires may have played a role in selecting for polymorphisms like those influencing dopamine and sensorimotor gating and other aspects of human cognitive evolution. Thus, the importance of human "fire fascination," as Fessler calls it, is only hinted at by the quaintness of the Yule log or the serenity of yogic candle meditation.[23]

Firelight Distorts Our Sensory Perceptions

Using fire to extend the day challenges our natural tendency to calm down, with the lights, sounds, and surrounding darkness triggering our wariness. The dissonance created can be emulated using the "strange-face-in-the-mirror" illusion.[24] Several years ago, I had students come up with experiential activities for selections from Julian Paul Keenan's *The Face in the Mirror*, which we read because of its exploration of the mirror test and self-recognition discussed in the previous chapter.[25] I had booked a dance studio at my institution in which to teach this class session so we could be surrounded by mirrors. I wanted the students to have increased awareness of themselves as we discussed this work and the significance of mirror self-recognition—to reflect on reflecting, as it were. It was fun to sit there awkwardly as most of the students tried to avoid looking at themselves in the mirrors. I love visual awareness tricks and use several in class. We played games culled from *Scientific American Mind*, when neuroscientist Vilayanur Ramachandran was editor and would feature an optical illusion in each issue (e.g., replicating phantom limb therapy by typing in a mirror box so it looks like typing with two arms), often making ourselves uncomfortable. One group of students took it further by replicating a child's game that had been explored by Giovanni Caputo, which he called the "strange-face-in-the mirror illusion."[26] Some may be familiar with this as a game called "Bloody Mary." To play this game, you hold a candle in front of you and walk into a dark room with a mirror, where you stare into your own eyes in the mirror for two minutes. The flickering candlelight messes with visual feature detectors in our optic system, and your face starts to do crazy things. When I tried it, everything on my face seemed to move around. At one point, the outlines around my eyebrows, mustache, goatee, and sideburns vanished. It looked like I had grown hair all over my face like a werewolf!

Charles Darwin recognized that human control of fire was among the most significant and defining aspects of human evolution, but even his great skill at broad and deep synthesis only scratched the surface in understanding fire's influence on us.[27] Fires have been critical in human evolution, enabling human ancestors to extend the day, provide themselves warmth, hunt more effectively, and, probably most profoundly, break down proteins and make them more easily digestible through cooking to quickly feed our growing brains.[28] In cooking food and gathering around fires for other social functions, a scenario developed in which human cognition and social behavior could have been influenced. Perpetually staffing a fire would have given ancestors a lot of bonding time and exerted selective pressure, favoring individuals and groups with higher degrees of cooperation and coordination in their fire maintenance. Furthermore, cognitive archaeologist Steven Mithen has suggested that *Homo sapiens* living floors were oriented around fires, with the various activities in which they were engaged taking place in close proximity to these fires.[29] This may have been critical to what comparative psychologist Michael Tomasello refers to as the "ratcheting" of creativity—juxtaposing technological modes in the same visual space may have sparked cross-modal sharing that led to the metaphorical explosion of human creativity and innovation that characterizes the Upper Paleolithic period.[30]

Consistent with this, fires seem to stimulate transcendence, particularly in the dark. The flickering light and sudden popping sounds of fires distort sensory perceptions. These sights and sounds (and smells and prickling sensations of heat) may hyper-stimulate our evolved orienting response to novel stimuli, particularly in the dark, wherein our senses are aroused to maintain security. However, this micro-stress response is followed by a relaxation response that dampens alertness.

This on/off toggling may lead to neurotransmitter cascades that produce relaxation and the concomitant quiescent sensation associated with fire. Though we are only beginning to understand the interactions of these various mechanisms, dopaminergic tone, as outlined in an earlier section above, may influence hypnotic susceptibility and, by extension, relaxation response.[31] Dopamine is commonly associated with reinforcing beneficial behavior and feelings of pleasure, but it is also the basis by which endorphin (endogenous morphine) is produced. Endorphin is linked to nitric oxide production, which, as mentioned above, is implicated in vasodilation and the reduction in systolic and diastolic blood pressure.

The daily cycling of hormones like cortisol also plays physiological roles in readiness for relaxation. For instance, anesthesiologists must use higher doses earlier in the day to get the same sedative response as they do later in the day. We also exhibit ultradian rhythms (short, from a few milliseconds to 20 hours) in our daily lives, from the cycle of our heart rates and periods between needing another cup of coffee to hypnotic susceptibility and consciousness.[32] Thus, it is not just fire, but as Polly Wiessner suggests, the time of day at which people gather together around fire that may be crucial in best understanding its mindful effects.[33]

Are Those Yule Log DVDs as Relaxing as Real Fires?

Though it is impossible to test if our cognitive abilities really evolved vis-à-vis domestic fires, my research group has been studying contemporary variability in the relaxing influences of fire and trying to tease apart the factors that produce this effect. We've tested this over several years now. In our first study, we positioned subjects for five minutes in front of a computer simulation of a hearth or campfire without naturalistic sounds, smells, sensations, or tastes, with a blank computer screen as a control condition, using a randomized crossover design (all subjects experienced all conditions in random order). We measured relaxation response as change in blood pressure from before (pretest) to after (posttest) each experimental condition.

Initially, many people said that both conditions were relatively relaxing and, as the experiment took place in a lab on a college campus using mostly student participants, a nice respite from the stress of going to classes. The students' impression of relaxation was verified by pre-posttest decreases in mean systolic and diastolic blood pressure, though the decrease was statistically significant only with respect to systolic blood pressure in the fire condition.[34] However, without the sound of fire to accompany the visual flickering, people reported that their minds wandered. Moreover, among the demographic information we collected about predispositions for relaxation was a religiosity questionnaire. We later scaled it back to just a few critical questions, but, when it was more extensive, one participant said the questionnaire primed her to think about "what a shitty Christian [she's] been," and the fire made her worry about how she is going to burn in hell. Also, it became obvious that we needed to test more sensory modalities and the importance a multimodal immersion into a fire experience may have for relaxation.

To do this, we began varying the conditions, first by adding a sound component in headphones. Though people claimed it was still a bit weird as compared to a normal fire, by and large we found that people were still relaxed by all the conditions. So, sitting for five minutes in a darkened room and watching a soundless fire video, watching a fire video with sound, and staring at a blank computer screen are all relaxing activities. In fact, many people dozed off, which we noted because they startled slightly when we spoke to them. When I compared the pre-posttest decreases across conditions and controlled for things like sex and age, which have known influences on blood pressure, I found the fire visual with sound had a modest relaxation effect.

In a third iteration of the study, we extended the conditions to 15 minutes each and changed the control to better simulate the structural features of a fire, substituting an upside-down photograph of a fire for the blank computer screen to simulate the fire's colors and contours. The 15-minute sessions confirmed our previous findings and suspicions. Not only was the fire with sound more relaxing than the control or muted fire conditions, the average heart rate increased during the control and muted conditions. People were downright exasperated by the longer period of sitting without both visual and auditory fire stimuli.

All this seems to suggest that fire is a multisensory experience that envelops us, pulls our attention in, and facilitates our ability to focus. I think that the campfire or fireplace experience is so powerful because the visual flickering and crackling sounds engage our orienting responses, the warmth is cozy, the smell evokes associations with savory food, poking it engages us kinesthetically, and it is a wonderful social pivot. We can commune at a fire, engage socially in conversation, or sit in silence without awkwardness because there is something else to focus on. In many ways, this is similar to watching TV. As psychologists Robert Kubey and Mihaly Csikszentmihalyi point out, the form features (cuts, edits, zooms, pans) of television are very similar to the movements of a fire.[35]

Two follow-up studies of fire and relaxation response have been conducted. One was conducted by a Dartmouth undergraduate under the supervision of anthropologist Nathaniel Dominy using Bluetooth heart rate monitors to test the student's athletic team around a real campfire for the experimental condition and sitting in the dark for the control condition. As with our study of simulated fire, the student found a robust relaxation effect among her teammates with respect to the real fire but not to sitting in the dark.[36] My lab also conducted a study that further disaggregated the sensory aspects of fire. We posited that, if fire with sound is more relaxing, maybe that's due to the crackling sounds, like the low-grade euphoria associated with ASMR (autonomous sensory meridian response). We also sought to explore whether television fascination (and addiction, by extension) were a by-product of cognitive evolution around domestic fires.

We followed up on our previous study by running participants through 15-minute conditions including the visual and sound elements, the sound element only, the stationary upside-down picture of a fire, and one of three "TV" conditions (a video on careers in anthropology, a video about the study of culture, and a video about Moundville Archaeological Park). We measured participant predispositions for hypnotizability using the Tellegen Absorption Scale, which assesses hypnotic absorption.[37] In this study, all four conditions were relaxing according to both pre-posttest blood pressure changes and skin conductance, a secondary measure of relaxation stress administered among a subsample of participants. However, there was a modestly greater relaxation effect for both the fire with sound and TV conditions among participants with higher predispositions for hypnotic absorption. We note the modesty of the findings as an important caveat in scientific research. Statistical significance is often the coin of realm in scientific studies, but the real meaning is in the size of the effect. Small effects may have garnered evolutionary advantages on which selection could operate, but it is much less likely than on a large effect size. Thus, while we report these findings, these findings warrant replication with larger and more diverse samples of participants before conclusions can be meaningfully asserted.

Yet, these findings are unsurprising in some respects. I've never heard anyone claim that domestic fires are annoying. Almost everyone agrees they are relaxing. But why are they relaxing? Do fires engage our dissociative tendency and help us learn to self-soothe? Did natural selection actually favor a genotype associated with dissociation or relaxation, or does each human get retrained through developmental exposure and practice? Several scholars have begun modeling this evolution, which, though fascinating, is not strictly relevant to the thesis of this book. However, I recommend works by Matt Rossano and Terrence Twomey which explore the specific capacities likely to have been enhanced through fireside cooperation.[38]

In the next chapter I return indirectly to McClenon's ritual healing hypothesis, which explores the role religion has played in giving structure to dissociation and in amplifying and disseminating its effects and meaning.

Notes

1 Daniel M.T. Fessler, "A Burning Desire: Steps toward an Evolutionary Psychology of Fire Learning," *Journal of Cognition and Culture* 6, no. 3–4 (2006): 429–451.
2 Damian R. Murray, Daniel M.T. Fessler, and Gwen Lupfer, "Young Flames: The Effects of Childhood Exposure to Fire on Adult Attitudes," *Evolutionary Behavioral Sciences* 9, no. 3 (2015): 204–213.
3 Polly W. Wiessner, "Embers of Society: Firelight Talk among the Ju/'Hoansi Bushmen," *Proceedings of the National Academy of Sciences* 111, no. 39 (2014): 14027–14035.
4 James McClenon, "Shamanic Healing, Human Evolution, and the Origin of Religion," *Journal for the Scientific Study of Religion* 36, no. 3 (1997): 345–354.
5 Gordon G. Gallup, Jr., "Animal Hypnosis: Factual Status of a Fictional Concept," *Psychological Bulletin* 81, no. 11 (1974): 836–854.
6 Ibid.
7 Susan B. Powell, Martin Weber, and Mark A. Geyer, "Genetic Models of Sensorimotor Gating: Relevance to Neuropsychiatric Disorders," *Current topics in Behavioral Neurosciences* 12 (2012): 251–318; Raz Levin et al., "Hypnotizability and Sensorimotor Gating: A Dopaminergic Mechanism of Hypnosis," *International Journal of Clinical and Experimental Hypnosis* 59, no. 4 (2011): 399–405; Pesach Lichtenberg

et al., "Hypnotic Susceptibility: Multidimensional Relationships with Cloninger's Tridimensional Personality Questionnaire, COMT Polymorphisms, Absorption, and Attentional Characteristics," ibid. 52, no. 1 (2004); 47–72; Pesach Lichtenberg et al., "Brief Research Communication: Exploratory Association Study between Catechol-O-Methyltransferase (COMT) High/Low Enzyme Activity Polymorphism and Hypnotizability," *American Journal of Medical Genetics-Neuropsychiatric Genetics* 96, no. 6 (2000): 771–774; Pesach Lichtenberg et al., "Hypnotizability and Blink Rate: A Test of the Dopamine Hypothesis," *International Journal of Clinical and Experimental Hypnosis* 56, no. 3 (2008): 47–72.

8 Naama Goren-Inbar et al., "Evidence of Hominin Control of Fire at Gesher Benot Ya'aqov, Israel," *Science* 304, no. 5671 (2004): 725–727.

9 James McClenon, "The Ritual Healing Theory: Therapeutic Suggestion and the Origin of Religion," in *Where God and Science Meet: How Brain and Evolutionary Studies Alter Our Understanding of Religion*, eds. Patrick McNamara and J. Harold Ellens, 135–158 (Westport, CT: Praeger, 2006).

10 Michael James Winkelman, *Shamanism: The Neural Ecology of Consciousness and Healing* (Westport, CT: Bergin and Garvey, 2000); Wiessner, "Embers of Society: Firelight Talk among the Ju/'Hoansi Bushmen."; James McClenon, *Wondrous Healing: Shamanism, Human Evolution, and the Origin of Religion* (Dekalb, IL: Northern Illinois University Press, 2002).

11 *Wondrous Healing: Shamanism, Human Evolution, and the Origin of Religion*; "Shamanic Healing, Human Evolution, and the Origin of Religion."; Michael Winkelman, *Shamanism: A Biopsychosocial Paradigm of Consciousness and Healing*, 2 ed. (Santa Barbara, CA: Praeger, 2010); Michael James Winkelman, "Shamanism as the Original Neurotheology," *Zygon* 39, no. 1 (2004): 193–217; "Shamanism and Cognitive Evolution," *Cambridge Archaeological Journal* 12, no. 1 (2002); *Shamanism: The Neural Ecology of Consciousness and Healing*.

12 Melvin Konner, "Transcendental Medication," *Sciences* 25, no. 3 (1985): 2–4.

13 Kenneth G. Walton et al., "Psychosocial Stress and Cardiovascular Disease Part 2: Effectiveness of the Transcendental Meditation Program in Treatment and Prevention," *Behavioral Medicine* 28 (2002): 106–123; Kenneth G. Walton, R.H. Schneider, and Sanford I. Nidich, "Review of Controlled Research on the Transcendental Meditation Program and Cardiovascular Disease: Risk Factors, Morbidity, and Mortality," *Cardiology in Review* 12, no. 5 (2004): 262–266; Kenneth G. Walton et al., "Psychosocial Stress and Cardiovascular Disease. Part 3: Clinical and Policy Implications of Research on the Transcendental Meditation Program," *Behavioral Medicine* 30, no. 4 (2005): 173–183.

14 Herbert Benson, *The Relaxation Response* (William Morrow & Co. Inc., 1975).

15 A.J. Arias et al., "Systematic Review of the Efficacy of Meditation Techniques as Treatments for Medical Illness," *Journal of Alternative and Complementary Medicine* 12, no. 8 (2006): 817–832; R.P. Blankfield, "Suggestion, Relaxation, and Hypnosis as Adjuncts in the Care of Surgery Patients: A Review of the Literature," *American Journal of Clinical Hypnosis* 33, no. 0002-9157; 3 (1991): 172–186; John W. Hoffman et al., "Reduced Sympathetic Nervous System Responsivity Associated with the Relaxation Response," *Science* 215, no. 4529 (1982): 190–192.

16 Bruce S. McEwen, "Protective and Damaging Effects of the Mediators of Stress and Adaptation: Allostasis and Allostatic Load," in *Allostasis, Homeostasis, and the Costs of Physiological Adaptation*, ed. Jay Shulkin, 108–124 (Cambridge: Cambridge University Press, 2004).

17 Tobias Esch, Gregory L. Fricchione, and George B. Stefano, "The Therapeutic Use of the Relaxation Response in Stress-Related Diseases," *Medical Science Monitor* 9, no. 2 (2003): RA23–34; Tobias Esch et al., "Stress-Related Diseases: A Potential Role for Nitric Oxide," ibid. 8, no. 6 (2002): RA103–18; George B. Stefano and Tobias Esch, "Integrative Medical Therapy: Examination of Meditation's Therapeutic and Global

Medicinal Outcomes Via Nitric Oxide (Review)," *International Journal of Molecular Medicine* 16, no. 4 (2005): 621–630; George B. Stefano et al., "Endocannabinoids as Autoregulatory Signaling Molecules: Coupling to Nitric Oxide and a Possible Association with the Relaxation Response," *Medical Science Monitor* 9, no. 4 (2003): RA83–95; George B. Stefano et al., "The Placebo Effect and Relaxation Response: Neural Processes and Their Coupling to Constitutive Nitric Oxide," *Brain Research Reviews* 35, no. 1 (2001): RA63–75.

18 McClenon, "Shamanic Healing, Human Evolution, and the Origin of Religion."

19 Frans B.M. de Waal, *Chimpanzee Politics: Power and Sex among Apes*, vol. Revised (John Hopkins University Press, 1998).

20 Brian Hare, Victoria Wobber, and Richard Wrangham, "The Self-Domestication Hypothesis: Evolution of Bonobo Psychology Is Due to Selection against Aggression," *Animal Behaviour* 83, no. 3 (2012): 573–585; Brian Hare and Vanessa Woods, *Survival of the Friendliest: Understanding Our Origins and Rediscovering Our Common Humanity* (Random House, 2020).

21 Richard W. Wrangham, *Catching Fire: How Cooking Made Us Human* (New York: Basic Books, 2009).

22 John A.J. Gowlett, "Firing up the Intellect," in *Social Brain, Distributed Brain*, eds. Robin Dunbar, Clive Gamble, John Gowlett, 573–585 (London: British Academy, 2010); "The Early Settlement of Northern Europe: Fire History in the Context of Climate Change and the Social Brain," *Comptes Rendus Palevol* 5, no. 1–2 (2006): 299–310; John A.J. Gowlett and Richard W. Wrangham, "Earliest Fire in Africa: Towards the Convergence of Archaeological Evidence and the Cooking Hypothesis," *Azania: Archaeological Research in Africa* 48, no. 1 (2013): 5–30; John A.J. Gowlett, "The Discovery of Fire by Humans: A Long and Convoluted Process," *Philosophical Transactions of the Royal Society B: Biological Sciences* 371, no. 1696 (2016): 20150164.

23 Fessler, "A Burning Desire: Steps toward an Evolutionary Psychology of Fire Learning."; Murray, Fessler, and Lupfer, "Young Flames: The Effects of Childhood Exposure to Fire on Adult Attitudes."

24 Giovanni B. Caputo, "Strange-Face-in-the-Mirror Illusion," *Perception* 39, no. 7 (2010): 1007–1008.

25 Julian Paul Keenan, Gordon G. Gallup, Jr., and Dean Falk, *The Face in the Mirror: How We Know Who We Are* (New York: HarperCollins, 2003).

26 Caputo, "Strange-Face-in-the-Mirror Illusion."

27 Charles Darwin, *The Descent of Man and Selection in Relation to Sex* (London: Murray, 1871).

28 Wrangham, *Catching Fire: How Cooking Made Us Human.*

29 Steven Mithen, *The Prehistory of the Mind: The Cognitive Origins of Art and Science* (London: Thames and Hudson, 1996).

30 Michael Tomasello, "The Human Adaptation for Culture," *Annual Review of Anthropology* 28, no. 1 (1999), 509–529. This refers to the older use of the word "ratchet," which refers to the tool otherwise known as a socket wrench, not the current slang use, which essentially means "hot mess."

31 Lichtenberg et al., "Hypnotic Susceptibility: Multidimensional Relationships with Cloninger's Tridimensional Personality Questionnaire, COMT Polymorphisms, Absorption, and Attentional Characteristics."

32 Andrzej Kokoszka and Benjamin Wallace, "Sleep, Dreams, and Other Biological Cycles as Altered States of Consciousness," in *Altering Consciousness: Multidisplinary Perspectives, Volume 2: Biological and Psychological Perspectives*, eds. Etzel Cardeña and Michael Winkelman, 3–20 (Santa Barbara: Praeger, 2011).

33 Wiessner, "Embers of Society: Firelight Talk among the Ju/'Hoansi Bushmen."

34 Christopher D. Lynn, "Hearth and Campfire Influences on Arterial Blood Pressure: Defraying the Costs of the Social Brain through Fireside Relaxation," *Evolutionary Psychology* 12, no. 5 (2014): 983–1003.

35 Robert Kubey and Mihaly Csikszentmihalyi, "Television Addiction Is No Mere Metaphor (Cover Story)," *Scientific American* 286, no. 2 (2002): 74–80.

36 Dr. Dominy told me of this finding in February 2020, and we have since discussed collaborative research to build on these findings and integrating his expertise on primate sensory systems.

37 A. Tellegen and G. Atkinson, "Openness to Absorbing and Self-Altering Experiences ("Absorption"), a Trait Related to Hypnotic Susceptibility," *Journal of Abnormal Psychology* 83, no. 0021-843 (1974): 3.

38 Matt J. Rossano, *Supernatural Selection: How Religion Evolved* (New York: Oxford University Press, 2010); Terrence Twomey, "Domestic Fire, Domestic Selves: How Keeping Fire Facilitated the Evolution of Emotions and Emotion Regulation," in *Handbook of Cognitive Archaeology*, eds. Tracy B. Henley, Matt J. Rossano, Edward P. Kardas, 415–430 (Routledge, 2019).

5

RULES AND RITUAL IN CURBING COGNITIVE DISSONANCE

The Wrong Holy Ghost

Several months into research for my doctoral dissertation, at a Pentecostal church in Poughkeepsie with a congregation consisting mostly of Jamaican immigrants, I encountered "Richie" and his wife "Amanda." They were in their mid-30s. Richie attended the church sporadically, and his sister and her children were members. Amanda attended a different Pentecostal church that he claimed to be a member of too. I first noticed him because he wore cornrows in his hair and flashy suits, which contrasted with the humble and chaste attire of most congregants. He came to dominate my attention when he started speaking in tongues and flailing about as though he were having an epileptic seizure. The church had recently formed a new gospel choir, and their exuberant performance was electrifying the congregation. When a song ended and the band stopped, the congregation kept clapping, maintaining the rhythm, and the singers reprised the chorus. This prompted the band to resume playing, though repeating a single musical phrase, creating a strong atmosphere of what one scholar terms "trance force."[1]

From around the church hall came staccato bursts of speaking in tongues accompanying physical spasms from other congregants. At the center of this activity, Richie was rocking jerkily in the pew. Amanda's son from another relationship, a boy probably around four years old, was next to Richie, and it looked like Richie's ecstatic flapping might clobber the child. Amanda, dressed noticeably different from the other women in the church as she wore no hat or leg coverings, removed the boy to the opposite pews of the church. When Richie's spasmodic movements caused his pew to tip backward with him in it, others moved in to catch him. A deacon supported Richie while several church elders closely monitored. Richie lay on the floor atop the overturned pew with his eyes closed and convulsed, uttering the same few sounds over and over like a phonograph arm on a skipping record.

DOI: 10.4324/9781003034483-5

Then Amanda began speaking in tongues and moved to stand over Richie, putting her hand on his chest. Meanwhile, two choirgirls possessed with the Holy Spirit circled the hall while holding hands and bending forward with their eyes closed, speaking in tongues over and over. The furor seemed to die down, but then another girl in the middle of the congregants erupted in tongues, triggering others to do the same.

It was an orgy of nonsensical sounds and jerking, flowing movement, church lady hats, ties, pointed shoes, sweat, and emotionally agonized faces. One of the choirgirls pacing the room moved to the pulpit behind the pastor and laid hands on him, speaking in tongues while he stood there watching the proceedings. An elder began rapidly pacing around the congregation with his eyes closed, praising Jesus and flailing his arms over and over. A woman behind me and a man who had moments before been talking with me casually in the foyer got caught up in the ecstasy and also began speaking in tongues.

After 15–20 minutes, the pastor interjected and asked the congregation to restrain their anointing, meaning to calm down the Holy Ghost flowing through them. This was an unusual rejoinder, as they usually deferred to the movement of the Spirit in the church, however long it went on. When they did not respond to his request, he started preaching over the noise, whereupon the congregation settled down—though with some tension in the room, which became more pronounced with the sermon he delivered. He spoke of cleaning one's own metaphorical house and not focusing on others. "Jesus shows his concern," preached the pastor, "by chastising those He loves. It is good to be chastised by God," he said, "because it means He loves and is paying attention to you. We have to be vigilant to be sure tongues are God and not the Devil; entire churches can be tricked." Without commenting directly on Richie but clearly insinuating something about his possession state, he said, "anointing is good. Tongues are good. But the Devil knows more tongues than all of us put together."

At the end of the sermon, the pastor made the typical altar call, wherein people who are ready to accept Jesus Christ come down to the altar to be prayed for. On this occasion he noted that the Holy Ghost was telling him "there is someone out there who wants Jesus in his or her life, but you can't get up out of your seat. That person needs to just get up and come down here now." Mind you, this is a frequent invocation and will sometimes be repeated multiple times until a number of people come forward to be prayed over. On my first visit, he said, "there is someone here who has an intellectual understanding of Christ and wants to know more. You need to stand up and come forward." I thought for sure he was calling me out and squirmed in my seat, concerned to avoid giving parishioners mixed messages about my intent there. A woman in front of me even turned and gestured for me to go forward. I did not, and the pastor never insinuated he was expecting me to throughout my nearly two-year study there. I heard it many times after and saw how effectively it compelled people.

Those who go forward may "tarry at the altar" while others lay hands on them. Tarrying at the altar is the intense seeking of the Holy Ghost during an altar call that is sometimes difficult to distinguish from tongues. It can involve intense dissociation but is not speaking in tongues per se. It is hard to discern when a person is speaking in tongues on such occasions amidst the volume of general ecstasy unless close enough—i.e., if one is among those laying on hands. Only those who have received the Holy Ghost can lay hands on others. This is a precaution to prevent harm being done, which can occur if demons transfer among individuals during such vulnerable moments.

Richie answered this altar call, and within minutes had fallen to the floor in what again might appear to be a seizure to an outsider like me. And again, others answered, and a fervent ecstasy broke out around the church, with people praising God and praying aloud in crisscrossing vocalizations. A group of tongue-speaking women including Amanda formed in the aisle. A female elder came toward Amanda to lay hands on her forehead, and at the mere touch, Amanda fell back with her legs akimbo, though seemingly unfazed by the fall. The women gathered around Amanda and laid hands on her.

Amanda appeared to be in a sympathetic trance, having some analog of Richie's experience—it is common among Pentecostals for a friend or family member to stand in as a surrogate for a spiritually or physically afflicted person and have healing hands laid on them. At the same time, a group in front was administering to Richie. One woman was repeatedly pulling something invisible out of him, as if those laying on hands were medics doing spiritual triage. When the group of women around Amanda dispersed, she got back up and went to the front to assist with Richie. However, within moments, the elders tending to Richie called an usher to escort her back to her seat. Amanda stopped speaking in tongues and just sat there with her dress clenched around her knees, appearing somewhat anxious.

An elder who had been on the floor with Richie's head in his lap requested the microphone. "Richie has stubborn demons in him that we are having difficulty getting out," he said. "Please gather around and help us pray for him. Richie is fighting a fight and can't do it without assistance." Several people went forward to help. The man who had been talking to me in the foyer pulled me aside to explain that Richie had been having some problems, so this was not a surprise.

Richie initially remained on the floor with the elders tending to him as though he had passed out, but, after a few minutes, rose to sit among them on the first pew who had been tending him as the pastor went to the microphone and announced, "I have never encountered something so difficult before in this church and have never had to say this to someone, but I just can't let it go anymore. You," he said, addressing Amanda, "have the wrong Holy Ghost." Moreover, he asserted, because she had the wrong Holy Ghost, she was impeding her husband's recovery.

"This is not me saying this," he pronounced in the cadences for which Black Christian churches are famous. "My Holy Ghost is upset and cannot abide by this and insists that I say something. So I cannot remain quiet. You, have the wrong Holy Ghost."

Both the pastor and Amanda appeared tense, though his demeanor was calm and respectful and hers angry and near eruption. Richie and the elders were, to my eyes, strangely nonplussed in watching the proceedings. Amanda stepped forward amidst the congregation and defended herself, announcing that she had been baptized in this church. Furthermore, she said, though she regularly attended another Pentecostal church in town, she had been to six Pentecostal churches altogether, and no one at any of *those* churches had ever told her she had the wrong Holy Ghost.

The pastor shrugged and replied that she should have those pastors call him so he could meet with them to explain.

"My husband has been like this for two days," she said, gesturing toward Richie, who sat placidly in the front pew as though meditating, "and I have been trying to help him. I admit I did some bad things in the past but not since I was baptized. I go to church, read my Bible every night, and do everything I'm supposed to do. How could I have the wrong Holy Ghost?"

The pastor replied plainly that his Holy Ghost was telling him that he must express this, or the problems would continue.

"I even asked my husband where he wants to go," she said indignantly, "and he said he wanted to come here, so I brought him here."

Right there in front of everyone, the pastor questioned whether Richie and Amanda had a good relationship and whether the relationship would work out. This turned out to be a clue to the drama. No one was taken aback by this inquiry.

When I interviewed Richie later, he admitted to me that the accepted practice before marrying in the Apostolic Pentecostal tradition is to consult the elders to receive guidance. Richie had gone against the warnings of the elders and had been married to Amanda outside the church by a Justice of the Peace. They had a very tumultuous relationship, and he had then divorced and remarried her three times over the course of two years! This violated church mores, which justified the pastor calling Richie out in front of the congregation. Richie apparently agreed, which explained why he sat quietly in the front pew without reaction.

While Amanda was defending herself to the pastor, other women had their hands up as if wanting to speak. The pastor held up a finger to quiet them, but they blurted out in tongues interspersed with condemning squawks of "wrong Holy Ghost!"

Amanda started to leave, putting on her coat and shoes and grabbing her son, but then she reconsidered and demanded, "You are a holy man saying I have the wrong Holy Ghost, and this is a holy building. I should be able to get the right Holy Ghost!" She re-removed her shoes and coat and went to the altar. I could no longer make out her words, but she seemed to be demanding the proper Holy Ghost by banging her hand on the altar. The elders appeared to submit and try, but after a few minutes, they gave up with a collective shake of their heads. Amanda stormed out of the church, son in tow, slamming the door as she went. Without missing a beat, another elder took the microphone from the pulpit and said, "God can only deliver what wants deliverance. People can only be healed or receive the Holy Ghost if they're willing."

After the service, Richie conversed with others jovially in Jamaican patois I could not follow, but he seemed unbothered by his wife's treatment.[2]

Shamanic Theory of Cognitive Evolution

As should be apparent because I am in this story, it is modern-day. And yet, contemporary Pentecostalism holds within it seeds of antiquity. Scenes like this mirror those reported by travelers and ethnographers from all over the world stretching back in time. Charismatic Christianity more generally, characterized as charismatic by the gifts of the Spirit (charisms) that are part of an experiential worship, may resemble the open marketplace of Gnostic practices competing during the early Christian-Roman period. The role of possession in these contexts is even older, resembling shamanic practices found around the world.

In the 1960s, religion scholar Mircea Eliade characterized spiritual healers in foraging societies as "shamans," adopting the term used by Tungusic language speakers (today known as Evenki) of Northeastern Asia and Siberia for their religio-medical practitioners.[3] Eliade suggested that all other modern shamanistic societies were related to these Tungusic speakers as part of a diaspora that, thousands of years ago, traveled across the Bering Strait into the modern-day Americas, and through links (substantiated to some extent by genetic evidence) to forager migrations throughout Europe and Asia during the Upper and Lower Paleolithic periods.

Cognitive and medical anthropologist Michael Winkelman, who has spent his entire career empirically modeling the characteristics and traits of shamanic cultures, proposes an evolutionary trajectory into which we can nest this Pentecostal vignette. According to Winkelman, shamanic cultures are characterized by their type of religio-medical care and leadership and by their subsistence mode—i.e., how they get their food. Shamanic behavior is associated predominantly with foraging and horticultural societies. The shamanic traits he sees as characterizing these cultures are, among other things, charismatic magico-spiritual leadership (the shaman), training that involves interaction with the spirit world, deliberate alteration of consciousness, an initiatory death-and-rebirth experience, soul journeys to commune with spirits, communal ritual activities, control of animal spirits, theories of illness involving soul loss, professional abilities including healing, and belief in abilities to do harm via sorcery. As subsistence patterns changed with the development of societies, usually as a result of population densities, religious behaviors changed as well. The same division of labor associated with food production and the storage and maintenance of food surpluses extended to the spirit realm with the emergence of an expert priestly class.[4]

Winkelman's shamanic theory of cognitive evolution proposes that the alteration of consciousness among Pentecostals has deep evolutionary roots, attested by these shamanic universals. Possible evidence of this antiquity is Upper Paleolithic cave art, which many scholars suggest is reflective of shamanistic rituals and altered state experiences. The purposes of such rituals are unknowable, but shamanic behaviors, according to Winkelman, mirror self-soothing behaviors exhibited by chimpanzees, such as drumming on trees and other objects during storms. These chimpanzee "rituals" (not to be confused with human ritualistic behaviors, as these chimpanzee behaviors lack conscious intention), resemble stereotypies or "stimming," the repetitive self-stimulating behaviors associated with autism and other developmental disorders in humans. Stereotypies are typical displays by all sorts of organisms when they are anxious and may be preparatory behaviors associated with fight-or-flight when a course of action to resolve the source of anxiety is unclear.[5]

Paleolithic peoples, or what are commonly termed "cavemen," likely engaged in activities that altered their consciousness, as suggested by anthropologists David Lewis-Williams and Jean Clottes in their studies of cave art. Though not all agree with these interpretations of the distant past that is based on scant evidence, it nevertheless seems likely that our human capacities for becoming hypnotically absorbed would not have just appeared recently, in historic times. Falling into and purposely nurturing hypnotic states have likely been part of the human condition forever. These states could have been created using behaviors that stimulate our internal biochemistry (i.e., stuff that causes our bodies to release, for instance, endogenous morphine or endorphin or endocannabinoids) as well as things we today would call "drugs," which stimulate our internal neurotransmitters. The use of fireside trance to self-soothe (discussed at length in the previous chapter) among early shamanic cultures, according to Winkelman, drew on primate capacities for reducing stress and aggression. As I will discuss more in Chapter 9, human use of plants to alter consciousness is a story of co-evolution that suggests one motivation for plant domestication efforts was to facilitate and amplify these hypnotic states. Altered states of consciousness are given meaning through the development and construction of culture. McClenon suggests that the development of sense of self and theory of mind alongside language led to narrative explanations for these experiences that attributed spiritual significance to them.[6]

The search for explanations for the unexplainable—undertaken through fireside storytelling—is likely the root of human mythmaking. Otherworldly experiences, wherein animals speak or exhibit anthropomorphic characteristics, are frequent in dreaming, spirit journeys, and other altered states, leading scholars to suggest that ancient peoples made connections between their waking and dreaming/spirit journeying lives to try to explain their place in the world. These sorts of non-human, anthropomorphic images—such as the "psychopomps" of Greek mythology that carried the souls of the dead—typify cave and rock art and religious imagery around the world.[7]

Music and dance are also main elements in shamanism, possession cultures, and trance. Music is central to Pentecostal worship and can make achieving dissociative states easier. The movement, vocalizations, and rhythm of music and dance all reflect biological capabilities and predispositions that, together, tend to bind groups through shared physical and psychological repertoires. Rhythm is central to life, from the pounding of our hearts and pitter-patter of rain to the insect and bird songs that have provided a soundtrack for all of primate existence. Music and dance are by-products bipedal locomotion (especially long-distance running), emotional vocal expression, and mimesis (mimicry), which also facilitate altered states of consciousness.[8]

Clinical psychologist Rachel Bachner-Melman and her colleagues believe that human dancing is linked to expression of a genotype for more efficient serotonin transport and arginine vasopressin production.[9] In their study, dancers were more likely than athletes to display this particular genotype and to score higher in hypnotic absorption. Arginine vasopressin released in the brain is implicated in social and sexual behavior, particularly attachment, mate-bonding, and other affiliative behavior. Interactions of serotonin and arginine vasopressin in the brain's hypothalamus are essential in communicative behavior and help us understand why dancing has such a prominent role in affiliative behaviors across cultures. This is as true of "dirty dancing" to signal sexual interest as it is of a father having a dance with his daughter on the day of her wedding to reinforce the persistence of her family ties despite joining a new household.

Similarly, music has a rewarding effect on human emotions that includes the release of oxytocin, a hormone associated with social bonding. Music has a non-linear communicative quality that lends itself to group coordination and collective intentionality. Neuroscientist Walter Freeman III suggested that meaning is the currency of brain dynamics, rather than information, and that music and dancing have been the basic biotechnologies for meaning-making and exchange among hominid brains for the past half million years. Adaptations and genetic changes in hominid limbic systems involving dopamine, endorphins, oxytocin, vasopressin, serotonin, and other hormones and neurotransmitters have likely been favored because they enhance social communication and self-regulation.[10]

A Brief History of Pentecostalism and a Religious Reification of American Exceptionalism

While I was in the midst of collecting the aforementioned Pentecostal data in upstate New York, I learned that an old punk rock friend of my wife had joined another nearby Pentecostal church, which intrigued me. I was collecting data to test my belief that, as Winkelman notes in citing my first published article,

> dissociation makes us better capable to act in our own self-interests by avoiding our ordinary socialized ego states and their intimate linkages to the desires of others [and that] dissociation as exemplified in spirit possession provides a further distancing from apparent self-interest.[11]

I was looking for a church where speaking in tongues occurred frequently and where the congregants would be willing to let me interview them and collect saliva samples.

Honestly, I was worried that no fundamentalist Christian group anywhere would allow me to do such research, so I had been going back and forth between the Poughkeepsie church with the great band and choir, a Mexican church with services in English and Spanish but heavily synthesized pop music, and a demographically mixed church with a so-so band and off-key singing. In addition to finding a place that would be willing to tolerate me, I wanted to find a church where I could endure working for months on end and sit through multiple hours-long services per week. Music matters a lot to me personally; therefore, my ability to understand the services and enjoy the music of the churches I would be working in for the next several years was of chief import.

I thought the church this friend attended might be a good compromise between my personal tastes and the religious behavior I was studying. As much as I wanted to expose myself to other cultural perspectives, I was tired of feeling uncomfortable and out of place all the time—a persistent obstacle in anthropological fieldwork. But the next time I ran into him, he and a group of like-minded brethren had left their Pentecostal church and initiated their own non-denominational charismatic services. They found the Pentecostal church too socially conservative and felt that a person should be able to have a beer now and then without violating doctrine. It had surprised me more that he had been a member in the first place, but, having collected data in the churches for several months by then, I'd also come to see their attraction. The next time I saw him, he'd stopped meeting with the non-denominational group and decided to pursue his own spiritual path. The group had started bickering among themselves and couldn't agree on which rules to follow. Even in the most organized of institutions, such human disagreements often lead things off the rails.

The story of the global Pentecostal Movement is similarly fraught. Pentecostalism is a somewhat new variety of Christianity that sprang up at the beginning of the 20th century. Most accounts trace the beginnings to Charles Parham or his student William Seymour in the United States, but Pentecostalism scholar and former minister Allan Anderson points out that a spirit of revival around the world in the late 19th and early 20th centuries morphed into Pentecostalism. Certainly in the United States, Pentecostalism is traceable to the preaching of Parham, who in 1901 was inspired to revive the spiritual gifts mentioned in the book of Acts in the Christian Bible. Agnes Ozman, a disciple in Parham's congregation in Kansas, was the first to speak in tongues under these circumstances. However, Parham was ridiculed by many locals, including former students, and his ministry in Kansas collapsed. He eventually moved to Houston, Texas and was preaching to African-Americans there, among them a young Black man named William Seymour. Parham sent Seymour to Los Angeles, California, where Seymour's charismatic preaching led to the Azusa Street Revival, which took place over several years, was visited by seekers from all over the world, and is also often considered a birthplace of the Pentecostal Movement.[12] A number of evangelists left that revival and started churches, seeding Pentecostal movements around the world.[13]

Many of the differences of opinion that led to the splintering of the Pentecostal Movement were present during the Azusa Street Revival, including a disagreement over the emphasis on speaking in tongues. Some think that any gift of the Spirit is sufficient to indicate that one has accepted Jesus as personal savior and asked for forgiveness. This is the case for movements like the Assemblies of God, where I have seldom witnessed people speaking in tongues. Others feel that tongue-speaking is *the* Gift sine non qua and must be manifest, which is the case for Apostolic Pentecostals and why I chose to work with them. Denominations also quickly broke along racial lines, with distinct Black and White traditions in the United States.

While Parham, Seymour, and Azusa Street were notable in the development of the global Pentecostal Movement, there were several revivals that provided the basis for an explosion of Pentecostal missionization. For example, the Holiness Revival Movement established the basic character of Pentecostalism several decades before the so-called spark at Azusa Street.[14] The Holiness Revival Movement, in turn, has its roots in Methodism, the belief of founder John Wesley in personal sanctification through Spiritual baptism, and a popular movement of revivals and camp meetings in the 19th century. Similar beliefs and practices permeated many religious movements of the period, and an emphasis on personal revelation or perfectionism extends to Quaker, Anabaptist, and other denominations around the world. A Welsh Revival in 1904–1905 spread to places like India and Madagascar. These revivals began with local people experiencing ecstatic phenomena and miracles of healing, and the missionaries likely helped assign Christian forms and meaning to these ancient dissociative behaviors.[15]

One of the remarkable aspects of the Azusa Street Revival was the mixture of ethnicities and genders in positions of influence and authority; and if the rise of Seymour as the Black leader of a racially mixed congregation in the Jim Crow-era United States is noteworthy, so too is the story of evangelist Pandita Ramabai in India. Ramabai was born and raised Brahmin but rejected her Hindu upbringing and married outside her caste. Her husband died two years after their marriage, leaving her to raise a daughter on her own. Ramabai was studying education in England and there converted to Christianity, after which she moved to the United States to continue her education. During that time, she toured the States, developing plans and raising money to establish a mission for women in India. She noted the democratization of denominational choice in the USA that contrasted both with the Hindu caste system of India and British domination through the Church of England. Ramabai established the Mukti Mission (mukti means "salvation") in 1889, which sent emissaries to revivals like those in Wales and another in Australia in 1904 to determine how a worldwide network could be established. What they found was a community of evangelical Holiness Movement pastors and missionaries all seeking to knit a world movement together.[16]

Thus, while Seymour and Parham before him may have been charismatic leaders (in both senses of the word), they did not start Pentecostalism from scratch. Many of the people who took "the Word" from Azusa Street to other parts of the world were already missionaries before the Azusa Street Revival. "Azusa Street was a place of pilgrimage for returning missionaries as word spread about the revival there," according to Anderson.[17] Many of the places where Pentecostalism spread already had converted populations and established Christian congregations. As missionaries went out from Azusa Street, the Mukti Revival was often the first port of call, facilitating rapid global cross-fertilization. Shifting to Apostolic theology with an emphasis on speaking in tongues, therefore, did not necessarily involve large or dramatic changes of philosophy or practice.[18]

Pentecostalism was the fastest growing and most successful Christian religion of the 20th century, according to some scholars.[19] Many suggest this was because of the direct access Pentecostalism provides to divinity. It has been especially successful among the poor, wherein the public demonstration of tongues vouchsafes a person with God.[20] One does not have to rely on intermediary humans to attest to one's worth, which was one of Parham's original complaints about denominational Christianity. God does this by speaking through the individual, which is an effective leveling strategy. Nonetheless, as Pentecostalism reached into the US middle class, tongues tended to be deemphasized as garish or unnecessary.[21] In my research, I observed that White middle-class charismatic churches in the US place much less emphasis on tongue-speaking, so it does not occur as often.

Pentecostalism is in some ways a revival of archaic Christianity. Christianity was once just one among many in the cult of Mithras, competing in a buyers' market where "pneuma" and altered states of awareness were a norm. Furthermore, there were many flavors of Christianity competing in terms of emphases. Religious studies scholar Elaine Pagels points this out in her discussions of the Apocrypha (the biblical books left out of the canonical Hebrew Bible) and, in particular, the Gospel of St. Thomas.[22] Gospels that raise up Mary as a godhead have been purged from the canon in favor of an androcentric emphasis. Similarly, speaking in tongues was suppressed among ancient practitioners. The main purge of tongues came from Paul in his messages to the Corinthians. He told them to stop pneumatic behavior so that Christians could distinguish themselves from the polytheistic pagan religions.

Pentecostalism is among many religions in the world that involve speaking in tongues and dissociation, but I have focused on it because it can be found around the globe. Thus, it makes a superb case for my argument that dissociation is not just a psychological function but an important cultural one too. In the next chapter, I extend this discussion and explore speaking in tongues as a trance state that, ironically, makes members stand out in society as oddballs so they can benefit from inclusion in a supportive social group.

Notes

1 Dennis R. Wier, *Trance: From Magic to Technology* (Ann Arbor, MI: Trans Media, 1996).
2 A version of this story was originally published in Christopher D. Lynn, "'The Wrong Holy Ghost': Discerning the Apostolic Gift of Discernment Using a Signaling and Systems Theoretical Approach," *Ethos* 41, no. 2 (2013): 223415–430247.
3 Mircea Eliade, *Shamanism: Archaic Techniques of Ecstasy* (New York: Arkana, 1964).
4 Michael James Winkelman, "Cross-Cultural Assessments of Shamanism as a Biogenetic Foundation for Religion," in *Where God and Science Meet: How Brain and Evolutionary Studies Alter Our Understanding of Religion*, ed. Patrick McNamara, 139–159 (Praeger, 2006); "Shamanism and Cognitive Evolution," *Cambridge Archaeological Journal* 12, no. 1 (2002): 71–101.
5 Michael Winkelman, "A Paradigm for Understanding Altered Consciousness: The Integrative Mode of Consciousness," in *Altering Consciousness: Multidisciplinary Perspectives*, eds Michael Winkelman and Etzel Cardeña, 23–41 (Westport, CT: Praeger, 2011).

6 Jean Clottes and J. David Lewis-Williams, *The Shamans of Prehistory: Trance and Magic in the Painted Caves* (New York: Harry N. Adams, 1998); J. David Lewis-Williams, *The Mind in the Cave: Consciousness and the Origins of Art* (Thames & Hudson, 2002).

7 Winkelman, "A Paradigm for Understanding Altered Consciousness: The Integrative Mode of Consciousness"; Winkelman, "Shamanism and Cognitive Evolution."

8 Gilbert Rouget, *Music and Trance: A Theory of the Relations between Music and Possession* (Chicago: University of Chicago Press, 1985).

9 Rachel Bachner-Melman et al., "AVP1a and SLC6A4 Gene Polymorphisms Are Associated with Creative Dance Performance," *PLoS Genetics* 15, no. 4 (2005): e1008135.

10 Walter J. Freeman, *Societies of Brains: A Study in the Neuroscience of Love and Hate* (Psychology Press, 2014).

11 Winkelman, "A Paradigm for Understanding Altered Consciousness: The Integrative Mode of Consciousness," 165.

12 Parham was later scandalized by attacks on his sexuality and financial mismanagement. As his influence waned due to these scandals, he bitterly denounced many other leaders of the new movement he had established.

13 Allan Anderson, "The Origins of Pentecostalism and Its Global Spread in the Early Twentieth Century," *Transformation* 22, no. 3 (2005): 175–185; *An Introduction to Pentecostalism: Global Charismatic Christianity* (Cambridge: Cambridge University Press, 2004).

14 Vinson Synan, *The Holiness-Pentecostal Tradition: Charismatic Movements in the Twentieth Century* (Grand Rapids: Wm. B. Eerdmans, 1997).

15 Anderson, "The Origins, Growth and Significance of the Pentecostal Movements in the Third World."

16 Allan Anderson, "Pandita Ramabai, the Mukti Revival and Global Pentecostalism," *Transformation* 23, no. 1 (2006): 37–48.

17 "Spreading Fires: The Globalization of Pentecostalism in the Twentieth Century," *International Bulletin of Missionary Research* 31, no. 1 (2007): 8–14.

18 Ibid.; Anderson, "Pandita Ramabai, the Mukti Revival and Global Pentecostalism."

19 Edward L. Cleary, "Introduction: Pentecostals, Prominence, and Politics," in *Power, Politics, and Pentecostals in Latin America*, eds. Edward L. Cleary and Hannah W. Stewart-Gambino, 1–24 (Boulder: Westview Press, 1997); D. Barrett, T. Johnson, and P. Crossing, "Missiometrics 2008: Reality Checks for Christian World Communions," *International Bulletin of Missionary Research* 32, no. 1 (2008): 27–30; David B. Barrett and Todd M. Johnson, "Annual Statistical Table on Global Mission: 2004," ibid. 28 (2004): 24–25.

20 R. Andrew Chesnut, "Born Again in Brazil: Spiritual Ecstasy and Mutual Aid," in *On Earth as It Is in Heaven: Religion in Modern Latin America*, ed. Virginia Garrard-Burnett (Wilmington, DE: Scholarly Resources, 2000): 219–234; *Born Again in Brazil: The Pentecostal Boom and the Pathogens of Poverty* (New Brunswick: Rutgers University Press, 1997).

21 Harvey G. Cox, *Fire from Heaven: The Rise of Pentecostal Spirituality and the Reshaping of Religion in the Twenty-First Century* (Cambridge, MA: Da Capo Press, 1995).

22 Elaine Pagels, *The Gnostic Gospels* (New York: Vintage, 1989).

6

THE BIOLOGICAL IMPERATIVE TO BELONG

Dr. Monkey Sex Goes to Church

The pastor of a local Pentecostal church told my student research assistant that he didn't want "Dr. Monkey Sex" coming into his church and telling them their beliefs were biological. Surprisingly, this was the first real confrontation I'd had with religious people because of preconceived notions they had about me. The pastor had looked me up on my department webpage and saw that I taught courses called "Monkeys, Apes, and Other Primates" and "Anthropology of Sex" and had given several guest lectures on primate sexuality. I explained to him that we were only interested in how God works through belief in Him to improve people's health, not in reducing belief to an essential biological process. Apparently reassured by my explanation of the motivations behind our research, he then asked me about some fossils his father, who was also a pastor, had found in Tennessee that he thought might be ancestral primates.

Before I started conducting biocultural research in Pentecostal churches, I feared the congregants would see horns sprouting from my forehead when I entered the building. A grant administrator at my doctoral institution confided in me before I started my fieldwork that she had grown up Pentecostal and predicted that I would be converted over the course of my study. One church member pulled me aside and told me that Jesus might not wait until my data collection was done for my salvation. Constant media coverage of the supposed culture war between religion and science led me to believe that my research would be fraught with resistance and suspicion on the part of my subjects. I believe, however, that the obstacles I had to surmount only made the study better, as they caused me to question preconceptions. Contrary to my fears, I met with little resistance in pursuing my research objectives. The administrator's prediction of my conversion also did not prove accurate, though I found out after the fact that at least some of the congregants

DOI: 10.4324/9781003034483-6

made assumptions about my beliefs in spite of the care I took to remain a detached observer of the services.

Some of the church members I worked with suggested I could carry their message to more intellectual circles that they felt were closed to them. Both of the main churches I worked at included people from all walks of life, who likely thought me another variety of believer, if somewhat heretical. Pockets of heretical Christians who spoke in tongues have persisted through the centuries, even after Paul the Apostle, who helped spread Jesus' teachings in the first century after his death, told the Corinthians to cut it out and speak in words everyone can understand (I Corinthians 14:2–19, King James Version). According to some of the Pentecostal elders who I chatted with week in and out, contemporary Apostolic Pentecostals—if not all Pentecostals—consider themselves the inheritors of such heretics. This attitude can lead to some dissent among the believers.

The kind of fracturing my punk rock friend's church experienced and that characterized the immediate aftermath of the birth of the Pentecostal Movement at the Azusa Street Revival (described in Chapter 5) still goes on today. In fact, the two churches I worked in experienced such divisions before, during, and after my time among them. The brethren of one church were primarily Jamaican immigrants living in Poughkeepsie, NY, but they advertised themselves as an Apostolic church with their doors open to anyone. The other church was in Kingston, NY, across the Hudson River and about 20 minutes away. The Kingston church was smaller, demographically mixed, and had a more family-like atmosphere. The pastor of the Kingston church was Nigerian, the assistant pastor Jamaican, and among the deacons were White and Black Americans and a man from India. Their music ministry was less talented than the Poughkeepsie congregation, but that made it easier for those without a spiritual gift for singing (like me) to take part. The Kingston congregation had a flourishing youth ministry and outreach, traveling over an hour each direction every Sunday to conduct a second morning service in Port Jervis, NY, before returning to Kingston for the Sunday evening service.

Though both churches called themselves Apostolic, there were prima facie differences. Some families who lived closer to the Poughkeepsie church chose to go to Kingston for services. Some of the parishioners of the two churches would pass each other on Sundays going in opposite directions to their respective churches. Figuring out the difference between the two churches was an important factor in interpreting cultural impacts on my investigation of endocrine or stress response to speaking in tongues.

The founders of the Poughkeepsie church had purposely set out to establish a church with "a Caribbean flavor," according to the pastor. Poughkeepsie is about two hours north of New York City, at the end of the Metro-North Hudson River train line. Much more affordable than towns closer to the city, Poughkeepsie is the farthest one can live on the Hudson line and commute to New York City to work, as I did initially. After September 11, 2001, many people moved out of NYC, including my wife and me. In the 1980s, Poughkeepsie had also been the northernmost reach of the NYC crack trade, as gangs worked up and down the train lines. The negative effects of the crack epidemic still plague Poughkeepsie today, while the surrounding areas conform to the model of New England quaintness associated with places like Amherst, Massachusetts.

When the future pastor's family first moved to Poughkeepsie from Jamaica via The Bronx, New York, he was not yet ordained, and they could not find an Apostolic church they liked. So, they invited a Jamaican pastor from the Bronx to come up to lead a congregation. That church flourished until his family talked him into going to seminary, whereupon tension developed over influence and leadership. Ultimately, this motivated their family to leave that church and start a new one, with him as pastor. This was the Poughkeepsie church included in my study.

Not long after I finished my fieldwork, there was another congregational split. The Poughkeepsie church had opted to lower some of the prohibitions in the church they said were "rules of man, not of God." The prescriptions that women wear head covering and that cosmetics be forbidden were not actually in the bible, the pastor and his wife said. They had picked these prohibitions up from the cultural influences of the Apostolic churches in Jamaica where they'd grown up and had brought such practices with them without inspecting those beliefs until they'd clashed with local practices.

This issue of prescriptive clothing is anathema to the direct experience of God at the root of Pentecostal theology, and these were among the differences between the Kingston and Poughkeepsie Apostolic churches that congregants cited. The requirement for women to cover their hair was specifically mentioned by members of the Kingston church as reasons they did not like the Poughkeepsie church. Thus, it appeared the Poughkeepsie church was trying to increase its appeal for more of its non-Caribbean community members. That seemingly small change led to a schism in the church, and a deacon who had joined while I was in the midst of my data collection left to start a new congregation. Several other members went with him, including his wife, who was the daughter of the Poughkeepsie church's assistant pastor and sister of one of its choir leaders. Several families were split right down the middle, with the wife going to one church and the husband staying in the other.

This idea that people can go to different churches to find what they're looking for is not at all unusual. When people move to new communities where there are many worship options, they typically shop around until they find one that's a good fit for them. I joke that choosing a church where I live, in Tuscaloosa, Alabama, is like deciding at which of the five burger joints at an intersection one is going to eat and wondering how they all stay in business. But there's a tension between wanting it your way and compromising some personal desires to fit into a community. According to the Poughkeepsie pastor, it's one thing to shop around, but once a person decides on a church, they should stay there. He believes that people need to learn how to work with others and listen to God's word, even when it's not convenient or what one wants to hear, as one's very salvation is dependent upon that commitment.

Getting in Your Own Way

"I have a lot of children, and I run a home school out of my house, so my stress is high. What if I had an argument with my husband before church? I don't want to make God look bad because my stress is so high," said one woman who declined to participate in the biological portion of my research. My objective at the churches was to test the influence of speaking in tongues on biological stress response with the working hypothesis that dissociation functions to reduce stress, despite its varied manifestations across cultures. Speaking in tongues takes place during dissociation in most cases, so I endeavored to quantify tongue-speaking, and compare it to biological and psychological measures of stress.

My plan was to develop a questionnaire that would assess how many times a participant had spoken in tongues in their lifetime as an approximation of how much influence it might have on stress load. At the time, good measures of chronic stress that could be easily implemented in field settings where people weren't super keen on being studied weren't yet widely used. Today I might measure hair or fingernail cortisol, which indicates the accumulation of hormone associated with fight-or-fight stress response, but that literature was just emerging. Salivary cortisol was already a standard measure of acute stress, and salivary alpha-amylase, another acute measure of stress but one that indicates the activity of the sympathetic nervous system—as does a sphygmomanometer, also known as a blood pressure cuff—was being tested in field studies. The advantage of salivary cortisol and alpha-amylase is that samples are relatively unobtrusive to obtain and collection methodology is not time-sensitive (that is, not affected by the "flow rate"—the amount of time it takes a person to spit in the tube—which requires that either the subject or an observer record timing data).[1] Research participants could sample themselves when I called to remind them and then bring me the sample tubes with minimal fuss. Both biomarkers can be extracted in a lab from a single spit sample. One disadvantage is that multiple samples need to be collected for any given day to be able to detect any variation resulting from cultural behavior (like speaking in tongues) in the context of a person's normal diurnal rhythm (daily cycle). To account for this issue, I called people repeatedly on Sundays and Mondays to remind them about sample times.

To provide context for the data I was to obtain, I first had to develop a culturally relative questionnaire, which required ethnographic study, interviews, and observation to understand the culture. The problem was that speaking in tongues is a more complex phenomenon than I had presumed. I knew this in my gut, but it was brought to light during the "wrong Holy Ghost" incident I related at the beginning of Chapter 5. This story seems outrageous on its face. How could a person have a "wrong" Holy Ghost? Isn't there just one?

As you might have guessed, "wrong Holy Ghost" is a polite way of saying, "you're being manipulated by demons" or, more bluntly, "you're full of shit." No one wants to hear either one of those. I asked the pastor how he knew Amanda was mistaken about being possessed by the real Holy Ghost. He told me that speaking in tongues is just one gift of the Holy Spirit (or charism, which is why they call religions that include such gift "charismatic"). There are many such gifts, including "discernment." There are also the gifts of interpretation of tongues, prophecy, and many others. Discernment is basically like a divine bullshit detector—one can tell when the Devil or his minions are working in the church. A non-Pentecostal might understand this as having a gut feeling or a bad feeling about something. One might say that people with the gift of discernment can "read the room" well or notice the subtext of interactions.

In this instance, the couple had been having trouble, and most of the community knew about it. Richie was trying to get his life together. He had been banned from the Poughkeepsie church because of his poor behavior and was trying to make amends and come back into the fold. He was also trying to work things out with his wife. But Richie had told the pastor that she was practicing speaking in tongues in the bathroom at home and church-hopping until she found one that accepted that she had received the Holy Ghost.

"So, that's the Devil?" I asked the pastor.

"Maybe a little bit Devil, a little bit her."

"So, it's not all Holy Ghost or all Devil?"

"No, they could both be inside of her, or many demons, or all her, or a combination. We can get in our own way and God's way as much as the Devil does."

"So, you knew before the service started that something weird was going to happen? Is that why you gave the sermon about speaking in tongues not being enough?"

"I didn't know, but I had an idea. I had talked with the young man and young lady. They are going through difficulties, and she is resistant to the resolution we suggested."

In the Pentecostal church, the elders vet a marriage before it is allowed to happen. Once that takes place, they encourage a couple to get married quickly, and then they're never supposed to get divorced. On the one hand, this sounds a little strict, but, on the other hand, they do intensive counseling of couples and do not bless a marriage that they don't think will work. It is reminiscent of arranged marriages in India as anthropologist Serena Nanda describes them.[2] Such arranging by elders takes pressure off a couple to show judgment they don't have enough experience to muster and ostensibly puts responsibility in the hands of experts. Then, once married, a couple is expected to work hard for a successful marriage. But Richie and Amanda didn't do that.

The question for me then became how to measure only the beneficial speaking in tongues. Events like the wrong Holy Ghost incident reinforce why ethnographic research is vital for biological studies. Familiarity with contradictions and frictions within culture not only problematizes but also, hopefully, leads to improvements in research design. After the wrong Holy Ghost experience, I found references by sociologists Brian Grady and Kate Lowenthal to what they've termed "excited" and "calm" speaking in tongues, which I'd observed without understanding it.[3]

Dissociation seems to be inversely related to emotional and physical maturity as it dissipates in frequency and intensity over time.[4] This maturation appears to correspond with increased self-awareness and mindfulness of others as part of developing greater balance and psychic integration over one's life. The excited version of tongues is what I described in the opening of the last chapter for the most part and is readily apparent. It is the type often caricatured in popular culture. Yet, the calm type is probably much more common, occurring among those most mature in the Spirit throughout worship services and especially evident when they are testifying or giving sermons. It comes and goes quickly, like a sudden shudder when a cold chill runs up your spine.

I also found that not everyone understood or agreed how speaking in tongues was supposed to come about. Amanda's practicing in the bathroom is not universally verboten among Pentecostals. Australian journalist Heather Kavan has written about the practice people undertake to be able to more easily receive tongues in her country.[5] However, the Poughkeepsie pastor felt tongues should come on naturally. He pointed out that practicing is just mimicking. His children observed tongues so much, they could easily mimic anyone, he said, which is not the same.

Still, it seems that cultural modeling is necessary and that it may vary among denominations or even church to church. Thus, while Amanda had observed tongues at a variety of churches and may have prepared herself as a vessel to more easily become possessed, the syntax or cultural order and arrangement of her behaviors and manifestation of tongues did not match the expectations of this particular church and its cultural model for appropriate behavior.

Seeking Social Validation

Josh Brahinsky is a labor organizer turned postdoctoral researcher studying the phenomenology of speaking in tongues among an Assemblies of God congregation in California. For several years, as part of psychological anthropologist Tanya Luhrmann's lab, they have been using an iterative process to get at the experience of tongues by asking participants to describe, say, the beginning or induction of speaking in tongues. "How do tongues start? What does it feel like? Describe how it comes on." The participants then answer, and Brahinsky and their team essentially reiterate the participant statement as a question, prompting further detail. This goes back and forth to get rich descriptions of the experience. Through this process, they have learned that most people fake speaking in tongues at first until they "drop in" to the real thing. There are a variety of degrees to this process of maturity and induction, but the bottom line is that there are both purposeful producing of tongues and possession trance. Those with more experience can induce the trance more easily. Brahinsky works alongside neuroscientist Michael Lifshitz with these mature tongue-speakers to measure glossolalia in an fMRI. They find that these mature states appear different from novice ones in brain scans.[6]

These distinctions highlight the terminology problem. What is the difference between this purposeful induction process, which sounds like speaking in tongues from the outside, and "dropping in," when God really seems to take over? One way difference can be ascribed is by using the term "trance" to describe the visible social experience. Trance states are visible and often serve social functions. There is a large family of dissociative types, but these types don't necessarily have shared biologies.

Trance is communicative. Its appearance conveys underlying meaning. The trance state is the visible manifestation of dissociation and serves a social function. No one can see the inner partitioning of awareness in the mind of another, but we can see a trance state. If you're in a trance, you're dissociating; but if you're dissociating, you're not necessarily in a trance. And it is possible to fake a trance. Trance states are part of a cultural grammar that are read in context.

In the questionnaire I developed for speaking in tongues among my Pentecostal congregations, I was able to ask about a variety of types of tongues a Pentecostal may have encountered.[7] Nevertheless, most people reported experiencing only excited and calm "Holy Ghost" tongues, or tongues that represented the manifestation of God in them. A few had experienced "backslider" tongues, which is what possessed Richie in the opening vignette in the last chapter. Backslider tongues is God fighting demons inside a person as they wrestle to return to the church (according to the Book of Matthew, seven new demons beset an individual every time they slide back into sin after being saved).

Using this culturally relative questionnaire, I was able to measure lifetime tongue-speaking experience as it related to possible benefits associated with salivary biomarkers of stress and arousal. I collected saliva samples four times per day on a consecutive Sunday and Monday among over 50 parishioners at the Poughkeepsie and Kingston churches. I called to prompt them to collect their samples at 10 AM, 2 PM, 6 PM, and 10 PM. This was the maximum number of samples I could reasonably ask them to provide, as they already wrinkled their faces at spitting in a tube, while getting enough to measure stress-related changes and distinguish stress indications from daily cyclical changes. I used a statistic called "area under the curve," which is an estimate of total cortisol produced on a day calculated by drawing a line between each coordinate on a plot and measuring everything under it. I tested for associations between lifetime speaking in tongues and other related factors and these daily totals of cortisol and alpha amylase.[8]

My findings supported my predictions for the most part. On days of service, people who are likely to be speaking in tongues are very active, moving around the church, singing, testifying, sweating. The stress and arousal measures for such individuals was relatively high on Sundays, consistent with this excitement. I predicted that those who had more lifetime tongues experience would show more active cortisol and alpha-amylase profiles on Sunday and have lower stress and arousal profiles on Monday. And that is essentially what I found.

I interpret these findings to suggest that people who speak in tongues more often are less susceptible to distressed responses in the face of daily hassles. This is consistent with studies of experienced meditators, whose meditation states are also considered forms of dissociation. Christopher MacLean and colleagues at the Maharishi International University (formerly Maharishi School of Management) in Fairfield,

IA, find similar benefits from Transcendental Meditation. In one, they found that the onset point of biological stress response is higher for experienced meditators. This suggests they don't get "stressed out" by daily hassles.[9] Herbert Benson and colleagues at the Benson-Henry Institute for Mind/Body Medicine at Massachusetts General Hospital have found similar results among those practiced in relaxation response, a practice derived from Transcendental Meditation. Furthermore, studies of mindfulness meditation practitioners show similar effects, suggesting that culturally moderated dissociation can be practiced and lead to changes in set-points of stress response and concomitant health benefits.[10]

Managing Impressions or Signaling Commitment

When I look back at pictures of church events where I felt comfortable taking photos—like baptisms where everyone was snapping them—I notice that the Poughkeepsie church appears to have Black and White members, but these snapshots don't capture the shifts in church membership. The church was founded to have a Caribbean flavor by an immigrant Jamaican family who over the years tried to broaden its reach by appealing to all people interested in the Apostolic tradition. They noticed that non-Jamaican initiates (Black and White) would show up, do the things it appeared they should be doing—coming down to the altar to show their supplication to Jesus, receive the Holy Ghost as evidenced by speaking in tongues—but then they would disappear after a few weeks. A group of photos I took shows two White women being baptized in the basement of the church. For Apostolics, this involves full water immersion, so they have a special tank. Since I went back and forth between two churches, I missed services here and there, but the day of their baptism was the only time I saw these women at the church. I also note that among participants in my study of stress was one White woman, who I recall speaking in tongues for the first time on the weekend I collected her saliva for the study and who I never saw again. Like the White people in my photos who I noticed because their whiteness made them a minority in the church, many new initiates are baptized, receive the Holy Ghost, but then do not return. Why?

Education scholar Valerie Young, who has studied imposter phenomenon or "imposter syndrome" for over 30 years provides one insight. People are less likely to feel like they belong if they don't share cultural characteristics with a group.[11] So why do these initiates go to the trouble of coming down for the altar call their very first visit, getting baptized, and speaking in tongues all at once? I think they're trying to make a good impression by doing the obvious things it would appear one does to join the church. In fact, if you ask the pastor how one joins and what the normal course of action taken is, it is something along these lines. However, the data suggest that the road to belongingness is a longer slog.

The same data I used to explore speaking in tongues and stress response provides some support for this claim. I say "some" because it was my first big study, so I threw kitchen sinks of questionnaires into my initial research design. At the beginning, the series of questionnaires took so long to complete that few people wanted to finish them. I also found them difficult to administer in the short time periods between church services when people would be willing to sit down and talk to me. Therefore, in the course of data collection, I started jettisoning questionnaires that were not strictly necessary to test my hypotheses. One questionnaire I initially included was the Balanced Inventory of Desirable Responding (BIDR), designed by psychologist Delroy Paulhus.[12] The full version includes three 20-item scales that measure separate factors for impression management, self-deceptive enhancement, and self-deceptive denial. Impression management is the stuff people do when they want others to like them, by playing up certain traits, and is considered a conscious tactic. Self-deceptive enhancement is an unconscious tactic people use to amplify their own desirable qualities. Self-deceptive denial is the unconscious playing down of negative aspects of one's personality. The self-deceptive denial scale has some items that tend to raise eyebrows, especially among conservative Christians, such as "I fantasize about raping or being raped."

It wasn't clear to most participants what the scales had to do with the study, since I did not have a clear sense of how I would use them at first either. When it became obvious to me that word would spread from the 20 or so who initially participated in my study that it was so long, I cut out the BIDR and other questionnaires that were redundant measures or not immediately useful for the completion of the dissertation. Fortunately, though, I did get those first 20 or so because it later enabled me to go back to those data and address this question of why some people came into the church and tried to fit in.

I compared socially desirable responding to constructs I call religious commitment signaling and faith signaling. By constructs, I mean I picked out the specific questions in my surveys that seemed related to signaling commitment or faith to others. I ran my survey data through the factor analysis function of my statistical software to ensure the factors I'd constructed hung together in a meaningful way, which they did. Then, I tested the proposition that trance states are the social manifestation of dissociation and carry cultural meaning for others. I used regression modeling to compare religious commitment signaling and faith maturity to impression management, self-deceptive enhancement, and the salivary biomarkers I'd collected for stress and arousal. Regression modeling is a way of seeing associations between two items—in this case, stress and religious commitment signaling or arousal and faith maturity or such combinations—in the context of other things that may have influences on those variables, such as age or ethnicity. For instance, ethnicity could control somewhat in this case for possible cultural exposure to the variety of Caribbean Apostolic Pentecostalism practiced in the church. Furthermore, through regression modeling, we can assess interactions between variables, such that when measures of one variable go up or down, it interacts with a second variable to influence the dependent variable.

Despite hypothesizing that there would be a different association between religious commitment signaling and impression management or self-deceptive enhancement, I was still surprised at the clarity of the results. They indicated that among those participants for whom impression management was high, cortisol (stress) was also highest and religious commitment signaling was relatively low. By contrast, among those whose religious commitment signaling was higher, impression management and cortisol were relatively lower. There were no statistically significant associations with alpha-amylase, the biomarker I used to measure the arousal of elevated heartrate caused by being active during the church service. There were also no associations with self-deceptive enhancement, which suggests that initiates were purposeful and aware of their efforts. The difference between impression management and religious commitment signaling was a statistically significant interaction that had an impact on cortisol only, or the stress they arrived at church with. I suggest this cortisol level is indicative of their preexisting states of anxiety.[13]

My ethnographic observations and expertise working in the church and knowing who these measures refer to and what was happening on the days I collected them lead me with a high degree of confidence to assert that the positive correlation between impression management and cortisol represent anxiety about fitting in. Those White people in my photos going down for altar calls and being baptized on their first or second visits were working hard to fit in, believing these were the things that would demonstrate their sincerity. Yet, the contrast with religious commitment signaling and cortisol, which is the measure that includes speaking in tongues and that cannot be easily faked by novices, indicates that the trance state of speaking in tongues is a chief signal of commitment and part of a cultural syntax in the grammar of group commitment.

Where dissociation may help reduce stress under appropriate circumstances, it is the trance state that is active in cultural grammars. When someone we're talking to zones out, that glazed-over look in their eyes tells us not what they're actually thinking about, but that we are somehow boring them or that their mind is elsewhere. It helps us understand something about our social interaction, not what is on the mind of that person.

In this chapter, I discussed why someone might be motivated to speak in tongues to show they belong and to get the benefits of membership, whatever those happen to be. In the next chapter, I take a step back again to look at the broader context of dissociation and its varied cultural forms. I pay particular attention to how culture and dissociation mold each other over time by tracking the history of dissociative disorders in psychology and anthropology.

Notes

1 Elana B. Gordis et al., "Asymmetry between Salivary Cortisol and Alpha-Amylase Reactivity to Stress: Relation to Aggressive Behavior in Adolescents," *Psychoneuroendocrinology* 31, no. 8 (2006): 976–987; Dirk H. Hellhammer, Stefan Wust, and Brigitte M. Kudielka, "Salivary Cortisol as a Biomarker in Stress Research," ibid. 34 (2009): 163–171; Clemens Kirschbaum and D.H. Hellhammer, "Salivary Cortisol," in *Encyclopedia of Stress*, eds. George Fink et al. (New York: Academic Press, 2007); J.A. DeCaro, "Methodological Considerations in the Use of Salivary Alpha-Amylase as a Stress Marker in Field Research," *American Journal of Human Biology* 20, no. 1520–6300 (2008): 5.

2 Serena Nanda, "Arranging a Marriage in India," in *The Naked Anthropologist: Tales from around the World*, ed. Philip R. Devita (Long Grove, IL: Waveland Press, 2000).

3 Brian Grady and Kate Miriam Loewenthal, "Features Associated with Speaking in Tongues (Glossolalia)," *The British Journal of Medical Psychology* 70, no. 2 (1997): 185–91.

4 Felicitas D. Goodman, *Speaking in Tongues: A Cross-Cultural Study of Glossolalia* (Chicago: University of Chicago Press, 1972).

5 Heather Kavan, "Glossolalia and Altered States of Consciousness in Two New Zealand Religious Movements," *Journal of Contemporary Religion* 19, no. 2 (2004): P171–P184.

6 Michael Lifshitz, Joshua Brahinsky, and T.M. Luhrmann, "The Understudied Side of Contemplation: Words, Images, and Intentions in a Syncretic Spiritual Practice," *International Journal of Clinical and Experimental Hypnosis* 68, no. 2 (2020): 183–199.

7 Christopher D. Lynn et al., "Glossolalia Is Associated with Differences in Biomarkers of Stress and Arousal among Apostolic Pentecostals," *Religion, Brain & Behavior* 1, no. 3 (2011): 173–191.

8 Ibid.; "Salivary Alpha-Amylase and Cortisol among Pentecostals on a Worship and Nonworship Day," *American Journal of Human Biology* 22, no. 6 (2010): 819–822.

9 Christopher R.K. MacLean et al., "Effects of the Transcendental Meditation Program on Adaptive Mechanisms: Changes in Hormone Levels and Responses to Stress after 4 Months of Practice," *Psychoneuroendocrinology* 22, no. 4 (1997): 277–295; Christopher R.K. MacLean et al., "Altered Responses of Cortisol, GH, TSH and Testosterone to Acute Stress after Four Months' Practice of Transcendental Meditation (Tm)A," *Annals of the New York Academy of Sciences* 746, no. 1 (1994): 381–384.

10 Herbert Benson, B.P. Malvea, and J. R. Graham, "Physiologic Correlates of Meditation and Their Clinical Effects in Headache: An Ongoing Investigation," *Headache* 13, no. 1 (1973): 23–24; John W. Hoffman et al., "Reduced Sympathetic Nervous System Responsivity Associated with the Relaxation Response," *Science* 215, no. 4529 (1982): 190–192; S.W. Lazar et al., "Meditation Experience Is Associated with Increased Cortical Thickness," *Neuroreport* 16, no. 17 (2005): 1893–1897; C.K. Peng et al., "Heart Rate Dynamics during Three Forms of Meditation," *International Journal of Cardiology* 95, no. 1 (2004): 19–27.

11 Valerie Young, *The Secret Thoughts of Successful Women: Why Capable People Suffer from the Impostor Syndrome and How to Thrive in Spite of It* (New York: Currency, 2011).

12 Delroy L. Paulhus, "Measurement and Control of Response Bias," in *Measures of Personality and Social Psychological Attitudes*, eds. J.P. Robinson, P.R. Shaver, and L.S. Wrightsman, 17–59 (San Diego, CA: Academic Press, 1991).

13 Christopher D. Lynn et al., "Religious-Commitment Signaling and Impression Management among Apostolic Pentecostals: Relationships to Salivary Cortisol and Alpha-Amylase," *Journal of Cognition and Culture* 15, no. 3–4 (2015): 299–319.

7

THE BIG UMBRELLA OF DISSOCIATION

The Biological Imperative of Deus Ex Machina

In the 1999 movie *Fight Club*, Edward Norton plays an auto recall specialist with serious ennui who seeks relief by attending support groups for sufferers of diseases which he does not have. With a character played by Brad Pitt, he becomes involved in a love triangle with a woman who also attends support groups under false pretenses and starts a club for fist-fighting as a release valve for men who feel powerless. There are lots of strange coincidences and implausible events in this noir drama, all of which are resolved by the revelation that the two main characters are in fact a single person suffering from the clinically rare dissociative identity disorder (formerly multiple personality disorder). Deus ex machina or "god from the machine" was the device in Greek plays by which a complicated plot could be resolved by the intercession of the gods (portrayed by actors who were lowered onto stage with a mechanical crane). *Fight Club* is among the best offenders of this cinematic approach.[1] I say "best" because it received so much more acclaim than other examples, becoming a cult classic. It is an "offender" because it skews the popular perception of the disorder, though I acknowledge that such distortions are pro forma in art and media to reduce complex phenomena to sharable narrative or impressionistic forms.

I learned about deus ex machina in a college classics course around the time I started studying dissociation, during which I also enjoyed the guilty pleasure of watching *One Life to Live*. Victoria Lord, one of the mainstays of the soap opera, suffered from dissociative identity disorder. I thought it was uncanny that something I was right then reading about was depicted on this show until I began to see it over

DOI: 10.4324/9781003034483-7

and over in popular depictions, far out of proportion with the disorder's real-world occurrence rate. According to the Victoria Lord Wikipedia page, the character

> weathers widowhood (three times), divorce (four times), a brain aneurysm, a near-death out-of-body experience (three times), being shot (two times), sent to jail, suffering a stroke, breast cancer, rape, a heart attack, heart disease, a heart transplant, the abduction of three of her five children as infants, the deaths of two siblings, and the death of her daughter from lupus. Most notably, she suffers recurring bouts with dissociative identity disorder throughout the show narrative.

What else but dissociative identity disorder could explain the implausibility that this person could possibly still be alive and kicking?

Part of the attraction of soap operas, which are patently ridiculous, is that they satisfy a human imperative for gossip. As social animals, we need news of what's going on in our community—who is doing what, who is desirable or undesirable, which behaviors meet with approval or disapproval—to help us figure out how to find mates, impress friends, maintain health and social status, and so on. Retired professor of evolutionary and experimental psychology Robin Dunbar proposes that language may have evolved in hominids as primate group sizes became too large to manage coalition-oriented information by tactile and gestural communication alone.[2] This need has driven human interest in the development of media so that much of our gossip now comes from other means than through our local, direct social network. Moreover, this biological imperative is tickled as much by mock gossip as by real gossip, so long as we're able to put the story in context. We can feel closer and more connected to fictional characters we watch on television or read about than our own families because of the continual stream available through multimedia platforms. This phenomenon is termed "parasocial interaction" or "parasocial relationships" and was first noted by communications scholars in the 1950s.[3] Yet if a story has to go on and on with no end in sight, as with soap operas, storylines become hackneyed and ridiculous by default. Humdrum, boring, everyday-life does not tend to motivate people to tune in.

Psychological and Psychiatric History of the Dissociation Concept

The shift in entertainment from resolving plots via gods to explaining aberrations through a rare mental disorder mirrors the transition in the cultural view of dissociation. What was once anomalous behavior attributed to some type of spirit possession has become a psychiatric disorder in need of clinical treatment. Psychiatrist and medical historian Henri Ellenberger traced the transition in belief of spirit and demon possession to dissociative disorders as consistent with the adoption of Enlightenment thinking. This same transition undergirds the American and French Revolutions and other transformations in the cultural zeitgeist happening at the time. In fact, according to Ellenberger, the discipline of psychiatry developed in tandem with interest in hypnosis beginning with Franz Anton Mesmer in the 1770s. Mesmer thought there was an invisible force in all living creatures that could be manipulated, and the term "mesmerism" is often considered synonymous with trance or hypnosis.[4]

Hypnosis is a form of dissociation that also renders subjects more suggestible. The term hypnosis was coined to distinguish that characteristic of hysteria believed to be an actual neurophysiological phenomenon and not just a product of imagination. Many thought hysteria was largely the product of suggestion that was amplified by what was then variously termed "hypnotic trance," "hypotaxy," "dissociation," or "trance-like state."[5] Mesmer's work was officially suppressed in 1784, but popular interest in animal hypnosis or "animal magnetism" continued to flourish. In England and Scotland, doctors like John Braid (who coined the term "hypnotism") continued to explore its use for potential anesthetic relief during surgeries. At the same time, a wave of Spiritism swept Europe and the Americas. The tenets of Spiritism are that the spirits of humans and other living things are immortal beings that temporarily and sequentially inhabit bodies to achieve intellectual improvement. During its popularity, Spiritism brought séances and mediumship into a period of vogue.[6]

The first published case on dissociative identity (termed "double personality") was by Swiss physician Paracelsus in 1646, the year the bloody French Revolution began. Post-traumatic stress disorder is commonly comorbid with dissociative disorders, but neither disorder complex was recognized then. The reintroduction of hypnotic therapy back into mainstream psychiatry took place in France via neuroscientist Jean-Martin Charcot, who used related techniques with hysterical patients. In the 18th and 19th centuries, a variety of famous cases of what would be called multiple personalities appeared, though by the 1890s, popular opinion of hypnotic techniques in therapy once again fell on rough times as sensationalistic stage hypnosis led to the discrediting of medical applications.[7]

Mesmer's student Armand-Marie-Jacques de Chastenet, the Marquis de Puységur, recognized that patients showed different manifestations under hypnosis, but it was Jacques-Joseph Moreau who first used the term *désagrégation*, which translates as dissociation. Moreau said it was a splitting off or isolation of ideas or parts of the personality. Paul Tascher (known by the pseudonym Gros Jean) is believed to have first proposed that nervous disorders like possession states, magnetism, and automatic writing took place in such divisions of the personality.[8]

The development of the dissociation concept and diagnoses by a handful of key figures marked a new era of psychiatry. Among them was French psychiatrist Pierre Janet, who most fully explained and clearly articulated the connection between dissociation and hysteria. Neurologic illnesses, according to Janet, developed because of frightening or traumatic incidents in the remote emotional history of patients that are then pushed into the patient's "subconscious," a term Janet coined. Psychological delusions and physical symptoms form around these suppressed memories. Janet and many French clinicians viewed dissociation as a sign of mental illness rather than as a defense mechanism as Sigmund Freud and British colleagues believed at the time.

Janet was an extremely influential figure in both European and US psychiatry and interacted regularly with such luminaries as Freud, William James, and Carl Jung.[9]

Multiple personality is likely the most complex form of dissociative disorder because of its elaborate combination of psychological and cultural elements. Even in the 19th century, there were already several famous cases, such as Félida X and Louis Vivet, which attracted scientific and public attention that distorted their relatively rare occurrence. This attention likely inspired Robert Louis Stevenson's *Strange Case of Dr. Jekyll and Mr. Hyde* in 1886, which reinforced and provided a cultural template for the type of psychopathological manifestations of multiple personality that show up again 100 years later in movies like *Identity* and *Primal Fear*.

Around the time that Stevenson's novella became a bestseller, William James was giving lectures in the US on dissociative disorders and linking them to hysteria, like Janet. However, James suggested that the disorders occur because multiple sub-conscious personalities become displaced from positions as hidden guides for the persona and instead become different manifestations of the individual. In the early 20th century, American clinicians Boris Sidis and Morton Prince published books specifically on multiple personality. Prince was among the first to suggest that dissociation is not strictly a pathological mechanism but could also operate as a normal aspect of psyche.[10] Throughout the first half of the 20th century, dissociation was viewed both from a structural perspective, as comprising specific brain structures such as the subliminal consciousness, and in a psychoananlytic context, as a coping mechanism.[11]

In 1963, psychologist Herbert Spiegel began using the dissociation concept to describe a process of defense and also as a framework for understanding normal personality. Spiegel outlined a spectrum of dissociation–association and suggested that dissociation is a fragmentation in response to fear and anxiety.[12] Six years earlier, multiple personality had vaulted into US mainstream awareness again with *The Three Faces of Eve* by psychologists Corbin Thigpen and Herbert Cleckley and the Academy Award-winning depiction of multiple personality by Joanne Woodward in the film of the same name.[13] In the late 1960s, psychologist Arnold Ludwig distinguished dissociation from altered states of consciousness but in the 1980s was still wrestling with a question of what fits specifically into the dissociation concept.[14] As a concept, dissociation is an explanation of psychological functions happening on a neurological level, and it is likely impossible to encompass all the neurological potentials of the brain that may result in partitioned experiences in one term or model.[15]

In 1976, Sally Field starred in the miniseries *Sybil*, based on the bestselling book by Flora Rheta Schreiber.[16] The miniseries received considerable public attention because of Field's presence (she had previously starred in the popular television series *Gidget* and *The Flying Nun*) but also because it was the first depiction of child abuse on television. Nevertheless, the Sybil case was contrived, at least in terms of representing "naturally" occurring multiple personality.[17] Faking multiple personality for attention, fame, or to escape criminal prosecution has been as much a part of the phenomenon of dissociative disorders as is controversy around faking possession.

In the 1990s, Colin Ross proposed that dissociative disorders should include iatrogenic (healer-induced) forms along with factitious or faked forms. Aside from psychopaths trying to escape prosecution by pretending to have multiple personality disorder, patients presenting as having multiple personalities are all clinging to cultural templates of pathology to seek help for themselves.[18]

In the 1970s, Ernest Hilgard was a clinical psychologist exploring the use of hypnosis and developed the concept of "neodissociation" to describe the results of normative processes while maintaining a Janetian view of an unconscious aspect he called the "hidden observer." Hilgard's model held that cognitive pathways or networks could be independent of each other. Though the neodissociation concept has not really stuck, Hilgard's suggestion that dissociation includes things like denial and psychological automatisms (e.g., driving a car while daydreaming) has influenced contemporary dissociation concepts, including the one I outline in this book. Hilgard described this spectrum of experiences including dissociation as the norm, whereas dissociative disorders are merely extreme manifestations that capture public attention because of their aberrant natures.[19]

A watershed moment in the clinical study of dissociation came in 1980 when the American Psychological Association published the *Diagnostic and Statistical Manual of Mental Disorders, Third Edition* (DSM-III) and moved dissociative disorders from a sub-category of depersonalization to a new heading as Dissociative Disorders and changed Multiple Personality Disorder to Dissociative Identity Disorder. This distinction was based on the by then mainstream theory that only one personality can exist. Contrary to early views that nearly complete hidden personalities could subconsciously influence behavior of the conscious personality, contemporary clinicians view dissociative disorders as problems of normally integrated aspects of personality. The DSM-III moved Somatoform Dissociation—a physical manifestation represented by psychoneurological symptoms—to a separate heading encompassing conversion disorders, pain disorders, hypochondriasis, and body dysmorphic disorder, among others. Onno van der Hart and Martin Dorahy, both psychologists who specialize in treating dissociative disorders, point out a consistent shift since the 1960s toward a broad and encompassing dissociation concept.[20]

The Dissociation Concept in Anthropology

The dissociation concept has been used in anthropology nearly as long as in psychology and psychiatry because of the influence these disciplines have on each other. In the US, anthropologists have also been interested in testing and integrating Freudian psychoanalysis on the one hand and in understanding cross-cultural altered states of consciousness on another. Several 20th-century anthropologists, including Alfred Kroeber, Edward Sapir, Weston La Barre, and Georges Devereux, were trained in psychology and anthropology. Sapir frequently assigned the classics of psychoanalysis to anthropology students, and it was while training under Sapir in the 1930s at the Yale Institute of Human Relations that La Barre began integrating both. He also met Richard Shultes there, whose explorations of plant psychedelics instigated LSD research in the 1940s and 1950s. Shultes and La Barre conducted a study of Native American peyote use in Oklahoma in the 1930s, which led to La Barre's dissertation on the subject, after which La Barre received a postdoctoral position at the Menninger Clinic in Topeka, Kansas to study psychoanalysis along-side Georges Devereaux. In the 1950s and 1960s, after personal experiences with peyote, ayahuasca, and psilocybin mushrooms, all of which produce psychedelic experiences, La Barre became more interested in altered states of consciousness.

Along with Shultes, La Barre investigated the anthropology and archaeology of altered states and came to the conclusion that the shamanic practices of Siberia were equivalent to those he had observed in the Americas and established a global theory of shamanism. La Barre's thesis largely supplanted the view proposed by Mircea Eliade, a religious studies scholar from Romania who earned his PhD studying yoga and Hinduism and who founded the study of religion at the University of Chicago. Though not an anthropologist, Eliade's ideas remain prevalent in anthropological studies of shamanism and altered states of consciousness to date. In 1951, Eliade published *Shamanism: Archaic Techniques of Ecstasy*, which explored historical forms around the world.

Unlike La Barre, who would suggest that Siberian shamanism is a model type that mirrors other cross-cultural types, Eliade suggested that some of the common tropes of shamanism—e.g., initiatory illness and the shaman's costumes and drums—have a common source in the Paleolithic as the original religion that diversified as it moved around the world. A combination of these models is obvious in the current works of anthropologist Michael Winkelman and sociologist James McClenon, whose shamanic theory of cognitive evolution I discussed in Chapter 5. It was Eliade who introduced the Tungusic word *šamán* to English, which was translated as "shaman," to describe a specific type of ethnomedical healer in small-scale societies. The word, according to Eliade, should not be applied to just any magician or medicine person lest it lose its meaning.[21]

Despite becoming prominent in "ethnopsychiatry" during his time at Menninger's Clinic in Topeka, La Barre's friend Georges Devereaux considered possession and dissociation purely the signs of disorder, as he had been trained to think in Europe. In conducting psychoanalysis among the Mohave Indians, Devereaux used terms derived from psychoanalysis such as "schizoid" to describe cultural aspects of the Mohave and other groups, which led to considerable criticism over the years. His characterization of possession states as related to hysterical personality types stems from his psychoanalytic training and contributed to much of his work being dismissed in the US.[22]

The same residual influence of 19th century French psychological theory can be seen in the earliest writings of anthropologist Anthony F.C. Wallace. In 1956, Wallace mentioned dissociation as one of the factors that would undermine integrated "mazeways," his terms for the combination of routinized behaviors and neural pathways that constitute habits, personality, and individual roles within cultural matrices.[23] Wallace is perhaps best known for his concept of revitalization movements and for his telling of the story of Handsome Lake. Despite being one of the most powerful Native American conglomerates in the early colonial period, the Iroquois were divided by conflicting alliances during the Revolutionary War and eventually forced into a small area, becoming subject to widespread alcoholism, intracultural violence, and imminent cultural dissolution. Among the Seneca, Handsome Lake was a quintessential example of these afflictions, until he had a series of trance visions in which Lake learned what changes to make to save the Seneca, an effort that was largely successful during his life. The Seneca subsequently fell back into dissolution as the new US government continued pushing Native peoples into smaller and unhealthier situations.

The success of the Handsome Lake revival caught Wallace's attention, however, and he sought to explain what had happened during those trances that led to such wholesale and successful reform. Wallace proposed that a mazeway is the neurological, psychological, and cultural set of pathways that constitute an integrated society. In Handsome Lake's case, this series of pathways was simplified, much like a decision tree where there are just a few choices at every juncture. Lake's insight was in recognizing the changes that could be made in Seneca culture to improve their quality of life so that other traditional aspects could be maintained. For instance, men traditionally hunted and women planted, but Lake pointed out that becoming self-sustaining—and refusing the White man's alcohol—were the only ways the Seneca were going to survive as a culture.[24]

Wallace's reference to dissociation suggests that the widespread view of it was as a disorder. Dissociation was, he noted, evidence of the collapse of the mazeways and the need for resynthesis. Wallace had been inspired to go into anthropology after reading James Frazer's *Golden Bough*, which makes allusions to possession throughout its assessment of cross-cultural fertility rituals. Wallace's primary adviser at Penn State was Irving Hallowell, a renowned anthropologist who had been trained by Franz Boas.

Boasian ideas of holism and inclusion have been the greatest influence on American anthropology over the 20th and 21st centuries and complement the broad continuum model of dissociation. Several of Boas's students, including Margaret Mead, had set out specifically to test psychoanalytic ideas in vogue at the time. Wallace had also taken an undergraduate course in anthropology that specifically introduced him to then-current psychiatric and psychoanalytic theory. Hallowell is largely credited with developing the school of "culture and personality" in anthropology that examined the interactions between culture and individual and was considered somewhat controversial for his use of Rorschach tests in studies of the Ojibwa Native Americans.[25]

Along with Wallace, Hallowell trained several other anthropologists who contributed to the possession and dissociation literature, including Melford Spiro and Erika Bourguignon (though at his previous institution, Northwestern, in the latter case). Bourguignon was also trained by Boas student Melville Herskovits, who conducted some of the seminal anthropological studies of Vodou in Haiti. Bourguignon followed suit and is considered one of the founders of the study of the anthropology of consciousness because of her focus on dissociation, possession, and altered states of consciousness. It was Bourguignon who, from 1963 to 1968, conducted the Cross-Cultural Study of Dissociational States. Using George Murdock's ethnologic database, the Human Relations Area Files, to explore the presence of dissociation across cultures, she and her co-authors published "World Distribution and Patterns of Possession States." They found that possession occurs in 90% of the 488 cultures surveyed. This finding lent significant credence to Siegel's continuum model and helped displace the cultural bias of viewing possession behaviors as pathological. In 1973, they published *Religion, Altered States of Consciousness, and Social Change*; and in 1976, Bourguignon published *Possession*, a cross-cultural analysis of possession states using her own research in Haiti as the basis for her case that dissociation is not by nature a pathological phenomenon.

Bourguignon's student Felicitas Goodman drew on her academic heritage to first conduct a cross-cultural study of speaking in tongues and published *Speaking in Tongues: A Cross-Cultural Study of Glossolalia* in 1972. Goodman used Siegel's continuum model of dissociation to suggest that dissociation ranges from normal to aberrant and to put culturally appropriate forms like speaking in tongues in context. She then began a series of experimental studies of trance postures, drawn from archaeology and art, to test the Freudian interpretation that such states are coping mechanisms. Goodman collected a variety of postures observed across cultures, such as those noted by Eliade as resembling yoga postures, and had subjects replicate them to determine if they facilitate dissociative states, for which she found some support. Goodman's next study examined dissociation in modern cases of demonic possession, and it was her 1988 book *How About Demons?* that I first discovered as an undergraduate, setting me on this trail. By that point, Goodman had started a New Age healing retreat called the Cuyamungue Institute, where she continued her explorations of trance and healing.[26]

Since the 1960s, anthropologists have followed clinicians in veering away from a pure pathology model of dissociation. Most now argue that possession and dissociative disorders are different cultural manifestations of predispositions to dissociate. Patterns of belief are what give dissociation structure and meaning. In clinical use, dissociation is a psychological pattern of unconscious behavior developed at a very young age in the face of severe trauma. The DSM states that "the essential feature of the Dissociative Disorders is a disruption in the usually integrated functions of consciousness, memory, identity, or perception. The disturbance may be sudden or gradual, transient or chronic." There are five DSM dissociative disorders: dissociative identity disorder, dissociative amnesia including dissociative fugue, depersonalization/derealization disorder, other specified dissociative disorder, and unspecified dissociative disorder.[27]

In the DSM, it is acknowledged that dissociation is not inherently pathological, and a cross-cultural perspective should be employed in the evaluation of dissociative disorders because of the ubiquity and variety of dissociative elements in normal cultural practices throughout the world. However, clinical definitions tend to be deficit-oriented and imply an ideal for this integration. Anthropologist Morton Klass pointed out that it is the role of medical experts to define and treat illness, not wellness; psychiatrists define mental phenomena with the ultimate goals of diagnosis and treatment of mental health problems. Nevertheless, one must be aware of the inconsistent use of dissociation as a term and concept, viz. Hilgard, as it often implies pathology and does not distinguish "dissociation" from "dissociative disorder" or "pathological dissociation."[28]

Despite this sometime confusion, many recognize dissociation as a fundamental aspect of the human psyche. Indeed, this view was the basis of Janet's psychological model, which was displaced as the model for American psychiatry by Freud's repression model. Many definitions tend to emphasize this influence. For instance, hypnotherapist Yvonne Dolan, defines dissociation as "the mental process of splitting off information or systems of ideas in such a way that this information or system of ideas can exist and exert influence independently of the person's conscious awareness."[29]

While I agree with the essence of this definition, it suggests differences that are qualitative but not quantitative. All alterations of consciousness are some form of splitting off. Indeed, all neuronal action involves moving through myriad synaptic pathways. Consciousness and unconsciousness are dictated by what pathways are activated. Thus, it is often the degree of dissociative partition, from a neuropsychological perspective, and the outward or social manifestation of the dissociation that merits special attention. For this reason, anthropologist Rebecca Seligman and cultural psychologist Laurence Kirmayer label cultural studies of dissociation as the "anthropological-discursive" paradigm of research.[30] Anthropologists tend to focus on dissociation as a social, rhetorical phenomenon framed in relations of power, agency, social space, and embodiment, as a performance emic (practice rooted in cultural beliefs), and as an adaptation that is only pathological under extreme and often culturally relative circumstances. Following this anthropological-discursive approach, I don't presume the psychiatric ideal of integration as the norm and, indeed, suggest that a lack of integration may be a by-product of focused attention.

How Does Dissociation Differ from an Alteration of Consciousness?

In 1957, the Canadian psychiatrist Raymond Prince answered an ad to work in a psychiatric clinic in Abeokuta run by the pre-independence colonial Nigerian government and spent half a decade there, during which he was initiated into the secrets of witchcraft, sorcery, and curative drugs. Over the period of time Prince was in Nigeria, he concluded that Yoruban people there have just as many neuroses and psychoses as Canadians or Americans and that the magical treatments of witchdoctors are highly effective. It was Prince who identified and named the cultural syndrome "brain fag" I discussed at the beginning of Chapter 2.

While Europeans and North Americans may suffer psychological discomforts resulting from pressures of modernity, such as keeping up with the Joneses and work-life balance, the Yorubans Prince encountered were struggling with the pressures of polygamy with similar results. When a man would take a second wife, the first would become jealous. If the first wife was barren, she would often be socially stigmatized and take out her frustrations on the children of the second wife. As free education was introduced in Nigeria in the 1960s, a generation gap was developing between children and their parents, often leading to the cursing of children, a very serious thing because of strong beliefs in the power of curses. After this experience, Prince returned to Canada and worked at McGill University, which had become a hub for the study of transpersonal psychiatry (what others call cultural psychiatry).[31]

There is a long history of the study of altered states of consciousness and their influences on mental health. Archaeologist David Lewis-Williams makes a strong case that many of the shapes found painted deep in caves like Lascaux during the Upper Paleolithic ~40,000 years ago are depictions of visual percepts seen during altered states of consciousness.[32] Numerous findings of poppy and hemp seeds and depictions of drinking among ancient people in the historic and near-historic periods suggest use of these substances for their mind-altering properties.[33] Archaeologist Patrick McGovern has made significant advances in exploring the beverages of the ancients and played a role in instigating the craft microbrewing craze when he teamed up with Doghead Fish Brewery to produce the "Ancient Ales" line of beers based on re-creating past beverages extracted from chemical analysis of ancient vessels.[34]

It was in the 1960s that Siegel first posited the continuum model, and we see in Prince's attitude the acceptance of altered states of consciousness as a normative mental healing strategy in the appropriate cultural context. It was also Menninger Institute in Topeka, Kansas and McGill University where transpersonal psychology seems to have rooted. The journal *Transpersonal Psychiatric Research Review* had been started at McGill just a few years before Prince went to Nigeria. Psychiatrists, psychologists, and anthropologists have worked closely together in building transpersonal psychology. It is no accident that the Society for the Anthropology of Consciousness that Erika Bourguignon helped found, which is one of nearly 100 smaller specialized societies within the American Anthropological Association, was for its first decade or so called the Society for Transpersonal Psychology.[35] Prince hosted several conferences in the 1960s featuring experts on altered states of consciousness that resulted in edited volumes, one of which is *Trance and Possession States*. That book featured the first publication of Bourguignon's cross-cultural analysis of dissociation, Arnold Ludwig's article delineating the features of altered states of consciousness (which would be followed in the 1980s by a similar article specifically distinguishing dissociation characteristics), and Prince's own contribution on the potential of studying possession states using EEG.[36]

Ludwig's contribution was the first academic definition of altered states of consciousness, which was refined and further popularized by psychedelics researcher Charles Tart a few years later. Ludwig defined altered states of consciousness as

> any mental state(s), induced by various physiological, psychological, or pharmacological maneuvers or agents, which can be recognized subjectively by the individual himself (or by an objective observer of the individual) as representing a sufficient deviation in subjective experience of psychological functioning from certain general norms for that individual during alert, waking consciousness.[37]

Tart is one of the founders of transpersonal psychology, which includes the examination of spiritual self-development, religious conversion, mystical experiences, spiritual crises, and other sublime or unusually expanded living experiences. He simplified Ludwig's definition a bit: "Altered states of consciousness are alternate patterns or configurations of experience, which differ qualitatively from a baseline state."[38]

The primary difference from dissociation is that altered states of consciousness are a broader spectrum of experiences among which the dissociation concept is nested. To return to the discussion in Chapter 4, relaxation response is the consequence of dissociation, though not necessarily of all altered states of consciousness. Dissociation is a psychological function of stress response, be it the stress of trauma, culturally mediated stress, or even subtle, idiosyncratic forms. The valence of dissociation as a positive or negative experience (or adaptive/maladaptive) should also include a neutral state akin and, related to biological stress response, is basic in returning to homeostasis. Dissociation is a functional accompaniment or feature of eustress ("good" stress) as much as distress or "negative" stress and everything in between.

These good/bad and adaptive/maladaptive binaries are useful for discussion and operationalizing research studies, but, as psychologists Richard Lazarus and Susan Folkman point out, valence depends on personal and cultural appraisal and is very fluid.[39] This function in stress response distinguishes dissociation from non-dissociative altered states. Ludwig's 1983 definition of dissociation outlines seven functional modes for dissociation, including (1) automatization of certain behaviors, (2) efficiency and economy of effort, (3) resolution of irreconcilable conflicts, (4) escape from the constraints of reality, (5) isolation of catastrophic experiences, (6) cathartic discharge of certain feelings, and (7) enhancement of herd sense (e.g., submersion of individual ego for the group identity, greater suggestibility, etc.).[40] These are all stress-reducing by either minimizing stress or deflecting potential stressors. Sometimes this stress is framed in relation to issues of power.[41]

Consistent with this view of dissociation as inherently stress-related, psychologist John Schumaker calls dissociation a censoring system that "*filters* vast amounts of information in order to diagnose data sets that are potentially *noxious* to the individual…to greatly reduce the complexity of incoming and stored information in such a way that a sense of order is more likely."[42] The mechanisms of dissociation may partition alarming information or stimuli away from awareness or elevate the threshold for neuroendocrine activation in determining what the brain tags as alarming. In other words, there may be denial or selective perception of alarming realities *or* actual recognition of them but the ability not to "stress out," in which there is neuroendocrine activation of epinephrine (aka adrenaline), cortisol, and other "homeostats" and the feelings associated with fight-flight-or-freeze responses to stress. Dissociation enables people to simultaneously accept two sets of contradictory information, an ability termed "trance logic."[43]

The Dissociative Family of Experiences

One of the most common but underappreciated forms of consciousness alteration is everyday music listening. When I challenge students to develop projects
to explore consciousness alterations, studies of music are among the most common. However, few consider the role music plays as background, something that
aids us by enabling our minds to focus on what is at hand, perhaps blocking out
other stimuli, even of our own distracting thoughts, without necessarily even consciously attending to it. As ethnomusicologist Ruth Herbert indicates, striking
and phenomenologically rich experiences with music and the strong associations
people report of such music experiences make them more compelling foci of
research that are easier to operationalize in psychological studies, but in *everyday*
listening, our attention is not focused on a psychology experiment; it is spread
across an array of distractions.[44] Cultural theorist Michael Bull suggests that iPod
use, for instance, is "a purposeful way of managing consciousness."[45] While things
with strong emotional valence may be "catchier" or more memorable, we often
focus on these things as exemplars of everyday states because they are easier to
define and describe for study.

Dissociation has been described as comprising a continuum of experience. At
one end lie culturally instructed and ritualized types—structured by society—such
as the shamanic spirit journeys of visionary trance or the possession trance found
in the Caribbean—while at the other are the aberrant and pathological types like
dissociative identity disorder and demoniac possession. But where does music listening fit? Positions are determined by the degree to which a society approves of and
invokes dissociation. The forms that are taught as an explicit part of cultural belief
systems involve communities that converge expressly for possession ceremonies and
often dance, sing or chant, eat, drink, and socialize. At the other end of the spectrum,
dissociation is unconsciously structured by the individual. For example, victims of
dissociative identity disorder may feel stigmatized by their trauma or mental health
issues.[46]

While this continuum is not wrong, it is incomplete. It is generally represented as
a simplified linear model, though it has long been recognized as multi-dimensional,
and many theorists have attempted to address the confusion the unitary model has
caused by identifying different types of dissociation.[47] It might be better conceived
as a three-dimensional field or spectrum because its forms vary widely in cultural
integration, persistence, and intensity. But the intensity, frequency, and particularly
the context of dissociation will often determine cultural acceptability, such that
even acceptable forms like speaking in tongues, when done too intensely, too frequently, or in the wrong context, might be interpreted as pathological (or demonia-
cal instead of divine).

This model of dissociation is not a closed and coherent system; dissociation is
a biological capacity that is culturally and psychologically malleable. In Chapter
8, I go into more detail about the brain mechanisms that enable this diversity to
occur.

Notes

1 *Split* and *Glass* are more recent examples I had the pleasure to watch back to back on a flight to the Pacific, and I quite enjoyed them, but the recentness of the movie is beside the point.

2 Robin I.M. Dunbar, *Grooming, Gossip, and the Evolution of Language* (Cambridge: Harvard University Press, 1996).

3 Donald Horton and R. Richard Wohl, "Mass Communication and Para-Social Interaction," *Psychiatry* 19, no. 3 (1956): 215–229.

4 Henri Frédéric Ellenberger, *The Discovery of the Unconscious: The History and Evolution of Dynamic Psychiatry* (New York: Basic Books, 1970).

5 Ibid.

6 Ibid.

7 Ibid.

8 Ibid.

9 Onno van der Hart and Rutger Horst, "The Dissociation Theory of Pierre Janet," *Journal of Traumatic Stress* 2, no. 4 (1989): 397–412.

10 Morton Prince, *The Dissociation of a Personality: A Biographical Study in Abnormal Psychology* (New York: Longmans Green & Co., 1905).

11 E.T. Carlson, "The History of Dissociation until 1880," in *Split Minds/Split Brains*, ed. J.M. Quen, 7–30 (New York: New York University Press, 1986); Colin A. Ross, "History, Phenomenology, and Epidemiology of Dissociation," in *Handbook of Dissociation*, eds. L.K. Michelson and W.J. Ray, 3–24 (New York: Plenum Press, 1996).

12 Herbert Spiegel, "The Dissociation-Association Continuum," *Journal of Nervous and Mental Disease* 136, no. 4 (1963): 374–378.

13 Nunnally Johnson, Corbett H. Thigpen, and Hervey M. Cleckley, *The Three Faces of Eve* (Hollywood: Twentieth Century-Fox, 1957); Corbett H. Thigpen and Hervey M. Cleckley, *The Three Faces of Eve* (New York: McGraw-Hill, 1957).

14 Arnold M. Ludwig, "Altered States of Consciousness," in *Trance and Possession States*, ed. Raymond Prince, 69–95 (Montreal: University of Montreal Press, 1968); "Altered States of Consciousness," *Archives of General Psychiatry* 15, no. 0003-990 (1966): 3.

15 Onno Van der Hart and Martin J Dorahy, "History of the Concept of Dissociation," in *Dissociation and the Dissociative Disorders: DSM-V and Beyond*, eds. P.F. Dell and J.A. O'Neil, 3–26 (London: Routledge/Taylor & Francis, 2009).

16 Flora Rheta Schreiber, *Sybil* (Chicago: Henry Regnery, 1973).

17 Mikkel Borch-Jacobsen and Herbert Spiegel, "Sybil-the Making of a Disease: An Interview with Dr. Herbert Spiegel," *New York Review of Books*, April 24, 1997; Mark Miller and Barbara Kantrowitz, "Unmasking Sybil: A Re-Examination of the Most Famous Psychiatric Patient in History," *Newsweek*, 01/25 1999; Robert W. Rieber, "Hypnosis, False Memory and Multiple Personality: A Trinity of Affinity," *History of Psychiatry* 10, no. 37 (1999): 3–11.

18 Colin A. Ross, *Dissociative Identity Disorder: Diagnosis, Clinical Features, and Treatment of Multiple Personality*, Revised and updated ed. (New York: Wiley, 1997).

19 E.R. Hilgard, "A Neodissociation Interpretation of Pain Reduction in Hypnosis," *Psychological Review* 80, no. 5 (1973): 396–411.

20 Van der Hart and Dorahy, "History of the Concept of Dissociation."

21 Roland Littlewood, "Psychiatry's Culture," *International Journal of Social Psychiatry* 42, no. 4 (1996): 245–268; Emmanuel Delille, "On the History of Cultural Psychiatry: Georges Devereux, Henri Ellenberger, and the Psychological Treatment of Native Americans in the 1950s," *Transcultural Psychiatry* 53, no. 3 (2016): 392–411.

22 Dusan Kecmanovic, *Controversies and Dilemmas in Contemporary Psychiatry* (Transaction Publishers, 2011).

23 Anthony F.C. Wallace, *Revitalizations and Mazeways: Essays on Culture Change*, vol. 1 (U of Nebraska Press, 2003).

24 Ibid.; Anthony F.C. Wallace, "Revitalization Movements," *American Anthropologist* 58, no. 2 (1956): 264–281.

25 Wallace, *Revitalizations and Mazeways*, 1.

26 Erika Bourguignon, *Psychological Anthropology* (New York: Holt Rinehart and Winston, 1979); *Possession* (Prospect Heights, IL: Waveland Press, 1976); "Introduction: A Framework for the Comparative Study of Altered States of Consciousness," in *Religion, Altered States of Consciousness, and Social Change*, ed. Erika Bourguignon, 3–35 (Columbus: Ohio State University Press, 1973); "World Distribution and Patterns of Possession States," in *Trance and Possession States*, ed. Raymond Prince, 3–34 (Montreal: R.M. Bucke Memorial Society, 1968); Felicitas Goodman, "Phonetic Analysis of Glossolalia in Four Cultural Settings," *Journal for the Scientific Study of Religion* 8 (1969): 227–239; Felicitas D. Goodman, "Disturbances in the Apostolic Church: A Trance-Based Upheaval in Yucatán," in *Trance, Healing and Hallucinations: Three Field Studies in Religious Experience*, eds. Felicitas D. Goodman, J.H. Henney, and E. Pressel, 227–364 (New York: John Wiley & Sons, 1974); *Speaking in Tongues: A Cross-Cultural Study of Glossolalia* (Chicago: University of Chicago Press, 1972); Esther Pressel, "Umbanda, Trance and Possession in São Paulo, Brazil," in *Trance, Healing, and Hallucination: Three Field Studies in Religious Experience*, eds. Felicitas D. Goodman, Jeannette H. Henney, and Esther Pressel, 113–225 (New York: Wiley-Interscience, 1974).

27 Rebecca Seligman and Laurence J. Kirmayer, "Dissociative Experience and Cultural Neuroscience: Narrative, Metaphor and Mechanism," *Culture, Medicine and Psychiatry* 32, no. 1 (2008): 31–64; Association American Psychiatric, *Diagnostic and Statistical Manual of Mental Disorders (Dsm-5®)* (American Psychiatric Pub., 2013); Otto van der Hart, "Multiple Personality Disorder in Europe: Impressions," *Dissociation* 6, no. 2 (1993): 102–118.

28 Niels G. Waller, Frank W. Putnam, and Eve B. Carlson, "Types of Dissociation and Dissociative Types: A Taxometric Analysis of Dissociative Experiences," *Psychological Methods* 1, no. 3 (1996): 300–321; Morton Klass, *Consciousness and Dissociation: Paradigms Lost*, (Lanham, MD: Rowman & Littlefield, 2003).

29 Kenneth S. Bowers and D. Meichenbaum, *The Unconscious Reconsidered* (New York: Wiley, 1984); Martin J. Dorahy and Christopher Alan Lewis, "The Relationship between Dissociation and Religiosity: An Empirical Evaluation of Schumaker's Theory," *Journal for the Scientific Study of Religion* 40, no. 2 (2001): 315–322; Hilgard, "A Neodissociation Interpretation of Pain Reduction in Hypnosis."; John F. Schumaker, *The Corruption of Reality: A Unified Theory of Religion, Hypnosis, and Psychopathology* (Amherst, NY: Prometheus Books, 1995); Yvonne Dolan, *Resolving Sexual Abuse* (New York: W.W. Norton, 1991).

30 Seligman and Kirmayer, "Dissociative Experience and Cultural Neuroscience: Narrative, Metaphor and Mechanism."

31 Sidney Katz, "My Colleagues, the Witch Doctors," *Maclean's*, November 16, 1963, http://archive.macleans.ca/article/1963/11/16/my-colleagues-the-witch-docturs.

32 J. David Lewis-Williams, *The Mind in the Cave: Consciousness and the Origins of Art* (Thames & Hudson, 2002).

33 Mark D. Merlin, "Archaeological Evidence for the Tradition of Psychoactive Plant Use in the Old World," *Economic Botany* 57, no. 3 (2003): 295–323.

34 Patrick E. McGovern, *Uncorking the Past: The Quest for Wine, Beer, and Other Alcoholic Beverages* (Berkeley, CA: University of California Press, 2009).

35 It's also the society and publishes the journal where I first got my start attending anthropology meetings and published my first article.

36 Raymond H. Prince, *Trance and Possession States*, vol. 2 (R.M. Bucke Memorial Society, 1968).

37 Ludwig, "Altered States of Consciousness."

38 Albert P. Garcia-Romeu and Charles T. Tart, "Altered States of Consciousness and Transpersonal Psychology," in *The Wiley-Blackwell Handbook of Transpersonal Psychology*, eds. Harris L. Friedman and Glenn Hartelius, 121–140 (West Sussex, UK: John Wiley & Sons, 2013).

39 Richard S. Lazarus and Susan Folkman, *Stress, Appraisal, and Coping* (New York: Springer, 1984).

40 Arnold M. Ludwig, "The Psychobiological Functions of Dissociation," *American Journal of Clinical Hypnosis* 26, no. 2 (1983): 93–99.

41 For example, Lesley A. Sharp, *The Possessed and the Dispossessed: Spirits, Identity, and Power in a Madagascar Migrant Town* (Berkeley, CA: University of California Press, 1996).

42 John F. Schumaker, *The Corruption of Reality: A Unified Theory of Religion, Hypnosis, and Psychopathology* (Amherst, NY: Prometheus).

43 Martin T. Orne, "Hypnotically Induced Hallucinations," in *Hallucinations*, ed. Louis J. West (New York: Grune & Stratton, 1962).

44 Ruth Herbert, *Everyday Music Listening: Absorption, Dissociation and Trancing* (Farnham, UK: Ashgate Publishing Ltd., 2013).

45 Michael Bull, *Sound Moves: iPod Culture and Urban Experience* (Oxfordshire, UK: Routledge, 2015).

46 Eve M. Bernstein and Frank W. Putnam, "Development, Reliability, and Validity of a Dissociation Scale," *Journal of Nervous and Mental Disease* 174, no. 12 (1986):727–735; Bennett G. Braun, "Issues in the Psychotherapy of Multiple Personality Disorder," in *Treatment of Multiple Personality Disorder*, ed. Bennett G. Braun, 1–28 (Washington, DC: American Psychiatric Press, 1986); Felicitas D. Goodman, *How About Demons?: Possession and Exorcism in the Modern World* (Bloomington, IN: Indiana University Press, 1988); Colin A. Ross, "DSM-III: Problems in Diagnosing Partial Forms of Multiple Personality Disorder: Discussion Paper," *Journal of the Royal Society of Medicine* 78, no. 11 (1985): 933–936; R.E. Shor, M.T. Orne, and D.N. O'Connell, "Validation and Cross-Validation of a Scale of Self-Reported Personal Experiences Which Predicts Hypnotizability," *Journal of Psychology* 53 (1962): 55–75; Spiegel, "The Dissociation-Association Continuum."; A. Tellegen and G. Atkinson, "Openness to Absorbing and Self-Altering Experiences ("Absorption"), a Trait Related to Hypnotic Susceptibility," *Journal of Abnormal Psychology* 83, no. 3 (1974): 268–277.

47 Spiegel, "The Dissociation-Association Continuum."; J.G. Allen, *Traumatic Relationships and Serious Mental Disorders* (New York: Wiley, 2001); Richard J. Brown, "The Cognitive Psychology of Dissociative States," *Cognitive Neuropsychiatry* 7, no. 3 (2002): 221–235; Etzel Cardeña, "The Domain of Dissociation," in *Dissociation: Clinical and Theoretical Perspectives*, eds. Steven Jay Lynn and Judith W. Rhue, 15–31 (New York: Guilford Press, 1994); Emily A. Holmes et al., "Are There Two Qualitatively Distinct Forms of Dissociation? A Review and Some Clinical Implications," *Clinical Psychology Review* 25, no. 1 (2005): 1–23; Frank W. Putnam, *Dissociation in Children and Adolescents: A Developmental Perspective* (New York: Guilford Press, 1997); B.A. van der Kolk and R. Fisler, "Dissociation and the Fragmentary Nature of Traumatic Memories: Overview and Exploratory Study," *British Journal of Psychotherapy* qw, no. 3 (1996): 352–361.

8

DISSOCIATION, DEAFFERENTATION, AND TRANCE

Biolooping and Embodiment of Dissociation

Possession trance religions in the Americas took on different characteristics by combining the beliefs and practices of various groups of enslaved people from West Africa and those of their colonist enslavers. Haitian Vodou developed in Benin, West Africa among the Fon and Ewe and is marked by French Catholic beliefs; Santería grew out of the traditional religion of the Yoruba, molded to fit within Spanish Catholicism in 19th century Cuba; and Candomblé in Salvador, Brazil traces its roots to Yoruba, Fon, and Bantu-derived Africans enslaved by the Portuguese. During her research among possession trance practitioners of Candomblé in Salvador, Brazil, psychological anthropologist Rebecca Seligman took measurements of "cardiac autonomic regulation," a psychophysiological measure of total regulatory capacity. Seligman noted a higher rate of cardiac autonomic regulation among mediums than non-mediums, which she attributes to the deeper learning of trance behavior among them.[1] This echoes earlier research among the Umbanda groups of São Paulo, Brazil, by anthropologist Esther Pressel, who studied under psychological anthropologist Erika Bourguignon at Ohio State University and received her doctoral degree in 1971 based on this work. Umbanda also started in Brazil, merging lower-class Afro-Caribbean spirit possession with Spiritism, which was popular among upper classes in the 19th century.[2]

The large Brazilian cities of Rio de Janeiro and São Paulo are Umbanda strongholds, where informants told Pressel that space was so limited without government-sanctioned churches or meeting places that practitioners would have to train to become possessed at home. This manner of learning possession trance echoes Seligman's descriptions of Candomblé practices and is crucial for the sustainability of these religions that remain stigmatized as "primitive" or "animistic."

DOI: 10.4324/9781003034483-8

Culturally appropriate possession trance requires the type of repetition and practice that results in neuromuscular changes.

While I have talked little about dissociation triggers, it was a big focus of consideration in the 1960s. Those who felt dissociation was a manifestation of pathology, either individually or culturally, sought specific life events, experiences, or genetics to explain the extreme dissociation of disorders and possession. The other position was that these heightened manifestations were part of a continuum for which the triggers varied but that might be related to the stimulation of brain rhythms. This supposition was based on extrapolations from the writings of Eliade, La Barre, and others that became part of the zeitgeist of the 1960s counterculture and a limited number of experimental studies using the technology then available, such as EEGs. Today, with the general acceptance of the continuum model, the focus has shifted to how some people manifest aspects of dissociation more easily than others.

In cultural anthropology, the theory of "embodiment" is commonly invoked to indicate acknowledgment of a fundamental change in the body having taken place as a consequence of cultural practice. Much early embodiment theory discussed ipso facto the internalization of culture, but those scholars focused more on phenomenological aspects of embodiment and less on the biological specifics.[3] Anthropologist Carol Worthman addressed this gap, noting that when we are growing up, our bodies adjust to the world around us and the culture we live in—as the culture does to us and our capacities and interests in replicating and adjusting it. She distinguishes influences in this paradigm with regard to "dual embodiment" (continual interaction between biology and culture), "local biology" (relative impacts specific to a local environment), and "developmental indeterminacy" (changes resulting from growing up in specific environments).[4]

To explain how mediums could have elevated cardiac autonomic regulation as a result of their practices, Seligman suggests integrating the concept of "biolooping" into the embodiment framework. Bioloops are mental sequences that are repeated, a concept Seligman borrows from philosopher Ian Hacking, who proposed the term to describe how psychiatric illnesses become real through socio-cultural positive and negative feedback loops. Seligman uses the idea "as a way of modeling the circular and mutually reinforcing processes through which religious meanings and practices come to shape the bodily experience and functioning."[5] Though she also notes that this same principle applies to anything that is culturally embodied, not only religion.[6]

The concepts of embodiment and biolooping are useful in providing bridges among language, interaction, and the body in a way similar to Wallace's mazeway resynthesis model that I mentioned in the last chapter. Many bioloops are sequences of thoughts. The contents of these sequences are affected by cultural scripts, which are the discursive resources used to make sense of stimuli and responses. They render the looping we do cognitively consistent with the cultures we live and operate within through interpretation and attribution, as trances and other dissociative experiences must be explained using these same cultural scripts. As an example of how biolooping and cultural scripts interact, think of learning to play a musical instrument by focusing on well-known songs. I am learning to play guitar by picking out Otis Redding's "(Sittin' on) The Dock of the Bay." As a beginner song, it's a bit tricky because I can't rely on an "anchor finger" (one finger that stays in place) and must switch from G major to B7 to C major to A major for one part, and there are three different parts. I need my fingers to automatically form the chords without needing to think about them, which I can only facilitate by practice. But in my head, I sing the song and have heard it so many times that I have a natural sense in my body of the melody and know when I need to change chords, even if I have to pause a bit to get my fingers ready for the next chord.

Each neural circuit of this repeated sequence of a bioloop of hearing the melody in my head and playing the chords that generate that melody also create awareness of the positions of my hands corresponding to those sounds. With repetition, my hands begin to automatically form the chord shapes as I move them to the next position, and the melody of my playing begins to correspond with the one in my brain. This process of cycling bioloops connecting memory of a melody and the creation of those same sounds with my hands generating awareness through this iterative process is something like a light bulb receiving voltage. As cranking a generator creates more voltage and increases the light emitted by a bulb, so too repeated energy dedicated to biolooping increases awareness. Simultaneously, the awareness generated by previous bioloops attenuates but is not totally replaced. The sum of this residual awareness, if sufficient loops have occurred, will be experienced apart from the trance generating loop. This residual awareness exists in our mind decoupled from the looping that generated it and is experienced as a sense of derealization, depersonalization, or other altered state of consciousness. The feeling of being at a distance from ourselves, our senses, or our motor activities effects the dissociative state that is seen as a trance.[7] For me playing guitar, I experience this trance as getting into "the zone." I lose track of time as I enjoy creating this melody. The melody in my head and that emitted from the guitar by my playing will often blur in my awareness until I miss a note or fail to automatically recall the next part, at which point I snap back out of the dissociative state and begin paying attention to my fingers again.

The type and intensity of trance biolooping determine the type of trance experience. Light trances result from fewer repetitions, whereas more intense trances are produced via greater numbers of repetitions. Shorter bioloops involve small networks with fewer neurons, synaptic connections, and brain regions and vice versa for longer loops. This model allows for trances ranging in duration from milliseconds to a repeated thought sequence that may last for decades. Thought sequences themselves can be short—encompassing a single sound, movement, or thought—or be a long series or combination of sounds, movements, and thoughts. Changes in trance states take place through modifications of the elements in the looping sequence, or trances can be interrupted if such modifications decrease the energy in the neural loop.

The attenuation rate or gradual decline in awareness of each generated bioloop is also relevant in achieving trance, as rapidly attenuating awareness will not leave enough residual to build to a level sufficient to produce one. This is why hypnotists will promote a persistent awareness—to slow down attenuation rates—while they simultaneously reinforce a bioloop. Picture the stereotype of hypnotism involving a pocket watch set swinging back and forth and the slow intonement to focus on the swinging watch. Since the speed of looping is a factor in achieving trance, so then is the number of repeated elements in a sequence, as a shorter sequence of items in a loop is likely to cycle more quickly. To return to our intrepid author playing guitar, the fewer chords in a melodic section and the fewer sections in a song, the easier it is to achieve a "groove," which is synonymous with a trance. But only to a point, as overly simplistic melodies can prove too monotonous to focus on (a problem often achieved with syncopation, or slight deviations from the prominent rhythm).

Hypnotic induction in research and clinical settings is similar, with long and slow periods of focused attention encouraged by the hypnotist's slow and even intonements (e.g., the most commonly used are the Stanford Hypnotic Susceptibility Scale and Harvard Group Scale of Hypnotic Susceptibility).[8] The quicker a bioloop cycles, the less awareness of each loop is likely to attenuate, generating a trance more quickly. For instance, people who conduct rapid repetitive tasks often become dissociated from their work and can take on a hypnogogic appearance. People who feel rushed throughout an otherwise monotonous workday will report the same experience.[9]

Biogenetic Structuralism of Deafferentation

In the 1970s, before the advent of functional magnetic resonance imaging (fMRI), psychiatrist Eugene d'Aquili and anthropologist Charles Laughlin developed an interdisciplinary program called biogenetic structuralism. The philosophy of biogenetic structuralism is that universal human-like language, culture, and cognition are based in the organization and physiology of the nervous system.[10] There are several interesting threads of biogenetic structuralism, but the most prominent involved collaboration between neuroscientist Andrew Newberg and d'Aquili and continued by Newberg after d'Aquili's death in 1998. Newberg met d'Aquili while the former was a medical student at the University of Pennsylvania in the 1990s and brought his skills in neuroimaging to d'Aquili's research into the neural basis of culture and cognition.[11]

In 1993, d'Aquili and Newberg outlined a neurophysiological model to explain the transcendent state associated with passive meditation that can be generally applied to altered states of consciousness.[12] They explained this form of transcendence as the result of "reverberating neural circuits through tertiary association areas of the brain."[13] Though conceptually similar to biolooping, their key insight was the importance of deafferentation in the decoupling of sensation and awareness and of levels of awareness and insight from one another. Efferent nerves are those conveying information out of a region of the nervous system, while afferent ones bring information into an area (usually the brain or a region of the brain).

Deafferentation occurs through activation of inhibitory fibers that can block input into neural structures. For example, primary and secondary sensory areas of the brain's cortex are the first to receive incoming sensory information or translate said information, whereas tertiary areas integrate information from a variety of brain sources and give incoming sensations meaning. Primary areas are activated by one type of direct, incoming signal. The primary visual cortex responds only to signals coded as visual and that travel through optic nerve fibers, for instance. Secondary areas are usually close to primary areas for respective senses and are activated by multiple incoming signals. Inhibitory fibers active in the parietal-temporal-occipital area of the brain enable us to focus attention on specific objects and neglect others through the way this cortical region sorts sensory information. The tertiary areas receive signals from all of these areas and help us make meaning of these inputs. These tertiary areas can actively receive incoming sensory information and orient us to the external world or filter out sensory information if we are oriented internally. Thus, they are brain regions where abstract thought in part occurs.

Among the four primary association areas, d'Aquili and Newberg suggest the most critical to the feeling of "immanence" (being at one with the universe) may be the inferior parietal lobe, which they label the "orientation association area." They call it this because the inferior parietal lobe is responsible for spatial orientation. During meditation, inhibitory fibers dampen signals coming to this area on directives from the thalamus, which is like the brain's train depot. d'Aquili and Newberg repeatedly tested this model among various cultural forms of dissociative trance. Much of d'Aquili's earlier work used EEG, which enables researchers to see the degrees of different types of electrical waves active during various kind of activities. EEG studies consistently showed that alpha and gamma waves are more active during resting states. Alpha and gamma waves become less active and other types of brain waves more evident during active attention, physical activity, sleep, and other categorically distinct states of being. With the advent of increasingly sophisticated neuroimaging, Newberg and others have been able to see where in the brain such activations occur.

In comparing Buddhist meditation with a form of meditative prayer developed by Trappist Monks called "centering prayer," d'Aquili and Newberg observe activation/deactivation of alpha and gamma waves in specific cortical regions. The brain activities associated with these forms of meditation are different than observed during normal modes of consciousness, and the forms of meditation appear different from each other in their regional brain activities. Both forms of dissociation display increased activity in the prefrontal cortical area, which Newberg and colleagues call the "attention" area, as it correlates to the type of focus the Buddhist monks and Catholic nuns in the studies reported in association with their respective practices. Moreover, they both displayed the same deafferentation in the parietal orientation area implicated in the feeling of immanence. In their studies, the brain scans of people engaged in centered prayer also indicate more activation of the brain's language area and in the right hemisphere. These regions are involved in the rhythms of speech, among other things, so these differences are presumed to be related to the nuns' focus on words in the centered prayer, whereas the focus in Buddhist meditation is on clearing the mind.[14]

In 2006, Newberg published a study of speaking in tongues that was on the front page of the *New York Times* Science section. This study was different from the research with Buddhist meditators and the Catholic centered prayer practitioners in a couple of important ways. First, meditation and centered prayer are calm, relatively quiet activities, whereas speaking in tongues relies on ecstatic movement and singing. This presented Newberg and his research team with the logistic conundrum of conducting brain imaging of people moving around the room but also the issue of separating speaking in tongues from the dancing and singing it often emerges from and in the midst of. To overcome these challenges, they located subjects for whom speaking in tongues came easily and with a high degree of self-control. The study used single positron emission tomography (SPECT) analysis of five Charismatic Christians who were skilled at speaking in tongues. These research subjects came from a variety of Pentecostal and non-Pentecostal congregations. By measuring participants while they were singing and transitioning to tongues but with the self-control to sit still, Newberg and colleagues were able to establish that speaking in tongues is a distinct neurological phenomenon and to distinguish it from singing.[15]

What they saw on the SPECT scans of tongue-speaking was reduction of activity in the prefrontal cortical areas relative to other states measured in previous studies or the gospel singing among the same participants. The prefrontal cortical association area is the only one that has direct connections with all other association areas. Furthermore, the prefrontal cortex is strongly associated with self- and other-awareness. Deafferentation to this area can therefore be viewed as functional reduction of conscious awareness, which converges nicely with the Pentecostal possession belief that the Holy Ghost displaces the self during speaking in tongues.[16]

Trance States, or Slowing Down the Game

Tua Tagovailoa is an NFL quarterback who started for the Alabama Crimson Tide during the 2019 season. Having not paid much attention to American football before arriving at the University of Alabama in 2009, I have since marveled at the complex mental and physical coordination of quarterbacks. A friend once aptly explained American football to me as chess meets ballet, with tackling. As with chess, there are different roles and rules governing each position in American football, and a "play" is an orchestration of all 11 of one team's on-field players for a single move or "down" of a game. The offense alone could have anywhere from 40 to 60 plays per game. Football players need to know the play called on each down and what their respective roles are. The quarterback needs to know everyone's roles on every offensive play and have a mental map of where players will end up. For instance, with pass plays, the quarterback needs to know what route each receiver is expected to run because they throw to where receivers will be, not where they are. The defense also has plays called, with the objective to confuse the quarterback as to who is coming to tackle him versus who is covering receivers or runners. Once a play is called, the quarterback often starts a count with a fake verbalization or hand clap to get the defense to move a bit and tip their hand as to what they are about to do, at which point the quarterback may use verbal codes to change the play. Once the ball is snapped, the quarterback avoids being tackled while handing the ball off to a runner, looking downfield to see who to throw the ball to, or running it himself. All of this requires repetition so that plays and formations become second nature and so throws do not need to be aimed.

Tagovailoa is remarkable for his precision, as he is able to consistently throw the ball so receivers can catch it anywhere on the field without needing to change their stride. Sports commentators who previously played often speak of how elite quarterbacks don't aim when they throw. Instead, they automatically judge the arc, distance, and spiral of a football through the combination of natural ability with the thousands of repetitions they've had through years of practice and game play. This allows their attention to go to where tacklers are coming from and which of their receivers are open given the play that has been called. This football throwing ability is reminiscent of the infamous English archers who dominated 12th century battles during the Hundred Years' War. The archers' longbows were specially made and so powerful that they could only be handled by people who started training at 12 years old and built up special musculature to have the strength to pull them back. At six feet tall, longbows were so large that the arrow needed to be pulled to the ear to work, so archers could not aim but had to learn intuitively how to hit their targets, which also required skill developed through years of practice.

Such exceptional focus is termed "flow" state in sports, the arts, and other activities that involve an intersection between skill and training. Though they consider dissociation an essential aspect of this focused attention and flow state, sports and performance researchers tend toward the flow concept because it encapsulates more that seems special about the peak performance of sports or artistic performance, especially in front of audiences. Psychologist Mihaly Csikszentmihalyi, who developed the flow concept, and Susan Jackson, who studies of flow in sports and performance, acknowledge the importance of dissociation and absorption as key elements in flow.[17] Flow relies on training, automaticity of movement and muscle repertoires, and dissociation of one's ultimate goals or audience and noise to accomplish tasks. Another word for what fans observe as the hypnogogic flow state that enables fantastic feats of skill under immense pressure is trance.

Sports commentators who have played quarterback often note they can tell when a quarterback is in trance or "the zone" and conversely when they fall out of it from thinking too much, trying to do too much, or attempting to make up for being behind by scoring quickly. Great skill and practice need to be balanced with thinking just enough to recognize the defensive formation and deciding quickly how to proceed and with automaticity of action, not just in throwing and running but also, to a lesser extent, in the whole series of interactions and plays. Sports commentators note that when quarterbacks reach this balance point, the game has "slowed down" for them. What was once a complex and fast-moving chaos has become "second nature," a play that quarterbacks understand and can read. Their minds have sped up, creating the sensation of time slowing down. A good comparison is the movie series *The Matrix*, wherein the world slows down for Keanu Reeves' character Nemo so that he seems to dance around bullets with superhuman skill.

Neurologically, the expression "second nature" refers to an activity or ability that has been developed to the point that it is as though the person was born with it. This requires the development of neural pathways that operate reflexively, without cognitive deliberation, because thinking about things means neural signals travel farther and are processed by more brain areas. As behaviors or mental processes are repeated, neural connections are expanded and reinforced, so that what may have started as a small garden path of interconnected neurons in the brain becomes a superhighway of many hundreds or more dendritic connections among nerve cells. Whereas progress on a garden path is slower and requires attention to each step, a superhighway provides clear sailing to the point that driving may require little attention but is also fast enough that one misses details along the road.

During the latter part of his life, Francis Crick, famous as a co-discoverer of DNA, was exploring consciousness with neuroscientist Christoph Koch. Focusing on awareness of visual perception, they developed a model for this mobilization of neurons for attention they called "coalitions of consciousness." They pointed out that attention and consciousness are limited, but the possible objects of attention are much less so.[18] What people attend to is a factor of incoming stimuli and one's frame of reference. The more one knows about a thing, the easier it is to understand relevant sensory information and determine how to react. All of this requires neural processing among distributed specialized networks. Skilled quarterbacks mobilize a variety of sensorimotor areas to make quick decisions without being distracted by crowd noise, guilt over a previous mistake, or fear of being tackled. This coalition of awareness holds sway during a game or practice to optimize performance.

"Flow" States, or Dissociating on Another Level

Keith Jarrett is a renowned jazz pianist who started playing with Art Blakey in the 1960s, and by the 1970s was a bandleader in his own right. For the past 50 years, he has played hundreds of concerts in front of thousands of people per show wherein he spontaneously creates works of pure technical genius. Where does creativity like this come from, obviously given form by culture but with an improvisational capacity and technical precision that embodies cultural capital? We value such skill for its ability to entertain us and are entertained because the skill and its ineffable beauty impress us. And where does the perception of beauty come from in us as observers? We share the cultural values and access to those skills, giving us some insight into what is being achieved. Similarly, appreciating football or any other sport entails understanding the rules, lest it be a jumble. I admit I am not a jazz aficionado, but I love music and have mentioned my efforts to play it. Thus, I do understand the complexity of playing an instrument, of playing in conjunction with a band, and in playing for an audience. It is difficult enough to play a routinized song with precision and passion. Improvisation that is beautiful and satisfying to hear is on another level.

Jarrett is not alone in this ability, but has become one of the subjects of neuroscientist Charles Limb's investigations of creativity because of Limb's own love of jazz. For the past few decades, Limb has used improvisational jazz as the focus for fMRI studies to investigate the neural basis of creativity. What he finds should be unsurprising to readers who have made it this far, because creativity is marked by a flow state where a person stops thinking and just acts. Csikszentmihalyi and others refer to flow as synonymous with peak experience because those who have experienced flow describe it as feeling "in the moment" or most alive, where they stop thinking and act at their highest skill level. Limb and his colleagues find that the prefrontal cortical area involved in thinking things through and executing is less active during these flow states, and areas relating to autobiographical self and knowledge or skills one has obtained or refined are more active.[19]

While Limb remains humble about reading too much from limited research, his interpretations are consistent with comparative cases like that of Tagovailoa. Cultural beliefs, opportunities, and training while growing up complemented Tagovailoa's innate capacities for focusing his attention and completing sets of football-related behaviors to be successful in that realm. He also shows the charisma and leadership skills necessary to be a good quarterback, as quarterbacks are default team leaders. Tagovailoa has been of particular interest for this story because he is Samoan by heritage and culture, and, as cultural historian Rob Ruck points out in his book *Tropic of Football: The Long and Perilous Journey of Samoans in the NFL*, Samoan cultural mores make them very successful in the National Football League.[20]

Samoan culture is conservative, Christian, and village-based, with greater emphasis on obeisance to family, chiefs, and pastors than is typical in the United States. The US Navy administered American Samoa from 1901, when it became a US unincorporated territory, until the 1960s, when they were finally allowed to elect their own governor. American Samoa was economically developed during World War II for a Navy station there, which created thousands of jobs for natives. As with Christianity, the hierarchical organization and command structure of the Navy resembled Samoan culture, so convergence happened quickly and appealed to Samoan families. The Navy left after WWII but offered free passage to Hawaii for Samoan families who wanted to keep their jobs in the Navy. Samoan communities were established in Hawaii that maintain traditional Samoan values regarding family and church, with alliances to home villages in the Samoan Islands maintained at a distance.

Seventy years later, those value systems are still in place. Though the Tagovailoas were born and raised in Hawaii, their Samoan values remain evident. When Tua enrolled at Alabama, his whole family moved to Alabama to be together. In a September 2019 radio interview, Tua noted they were 15 minutes away from leaving after his first year at Alabama and going to a California or Oregon school, both of which have several top-tier college football programs with numerous Samoan players.[21] It seemed surprising that a promising player would consider leaving what has been among the top few best college football teams in the country for over a decade when it was likely he could be the starting quarterback the next season. Some American football broadcasters thought the Tagovailoa family was putting too much pressure on their children. However, having conducted research among Samoans in the Samoan Islands, Hawaii, and Seattle now for several years, the Tagovailoa family seems quintessentially Samoan. Samoans refer to the importance of *fa'asamoa* or "the ways of Samoa" frequently, which includes the subservience of young people to elders, submission to family, physical and financial support of family villages and churches, big meals of traditional and high carbohydrate foods, and Christianity.[22]

It may seem odd that I've spent the entire section about trance writing about football quarterbacks and flow instead of Vodou or other seemingly exotic manifestations that would catch reader attention. The reason I choose to write about football is to reinforce the normalcy of trance. We study the exotic and extreme to understand the everyday and subtle. There are many great ethnographies that describe trance states, several of which I have perused again in preparation for writing. But it seems too "othering" to use those examples when what we want to understand is the trifecta of dissociation, deafferentation, and trance. Trance is dissociation that others see. As much as I've written about Vodou, I've never seen a Vodun possession trance. Of course, I have seen many Pentecostal trances when people speak in tongues, which I have described to some extent, but there are other forms of trance I've seen too.

In his exhaustive book on music and trance, ethnomusicologist Gilbert Rouget compares trance to ecstasy in the manner I have compared dissociation to deafferentation to trance. He says that trance involves movement, noise, social context, crisis, sensory overstimulation, episodic amnesia, and no hallucinations.[23] The two pieces I want to stick a pin in are the amnesia, which is not true in all cases, and the sensory overstimulation. Memory is notoriously faulty, and memory during situations wherein there is lots of incoming stimulation is likely to be even more faulty. There is some complete amnesia in Vodou and dissociative disorders, which can be part of the socialization processes or the defense mechanisms of the brain, depending on the circumstances. However, I would argue that in most cases, such as when Tagovailoa is in the "pocket" created by his offensive linemen blocking the other team so he has time to find an open receiver and throw the ball accurately, there is such rapid mentation that memory does not have time to form. There is not enough time for the type of self-reflection that contributes to accurate memory formation. He is like a jazz musician in a trance relying on the skills he embodies, developed through biolooping processes, to produce new works of improvisational genius every time he goes to work. This lack of memory explains why so many quarterbacks default to talking about the team effort made in support of him when reporters ask how they stood in the pocket under pressure to make such magnificent throws. They don't remember how they evaded being tackled to make the throws.

The approach to trance used in this model best approximates that of psychologist Milton Erickson who developed a specialization in hypnotherapy.[24] In trance, says Erickson, there is a reduction in the foci of attention to a few realities rather than attention being diffused over our generally broad orientation to the here and now. The most common everyday trance is the one we usually call "zoning out" in the United States. A person's attention may be fixated on a question in the mind or a compelling image or scene that holds them in contemplation to the exclusion of other stimuli. They may tend to gaze off and get a faraway or blank look. Erickson supposed that everyday life vacillates between general reality orientation and the momentary microdynamics of trance.

In the next few chapters, I address more of the dark side of dissociation. One consequence of the anxiety and depression that seem commensurate with consciousness is the desire to put blinders on, stick our fingers in our ears, or put our heads in the sand. This can be done through self-deceptive obliviousness, as I address in Chapter 10, but drug and alcohol use are a more obvious by-product of dissociation, as I discuss in the next chapter.

Notes

1 Rebecca Seligman, "Distress, Dissociation, and Embodied Experience: Reconsidering the Pathways to Mediumship and Mental Health," *Ethos* 33, no. 1 (2005): 71–99; "From Affliction to Affirmation: Narrative Transformation and the Therapeutics of Candomblé Mediumship," *Transcultural Psychiatry* 42, no. 2 (2005): 272–294.
2 Esther Pressel, "Umbando in Sao Paulo: Religious Innovations in a Developing Society," in *Religion, Altered States of Consciousness and Social Change*, ed. Erika Bourguignon, 264–318 (Columbus, OH: Ohio State University, 1973); Esther Pressel, "Umbanda, Trance and Possession in São Paulo, Brazil," in *Trance, Healing, and Hallucination: Three Field Studies in Religious Experience*, eds. Felicitas D. Goodman, Jeannette H. Henney, and Esther Pressel, 113–225 (New York: Wiley-Interscience, 1974).
3 Thomas J. Csordas, "Embodiment and Cultural Phenomenology," eds. G. Weinn and H. Haber, 143–164 (New York: Routledge, 1999); *The Sacred Self: A Cultural Phenomenology of Charismatic Healing* (Berkeley, CA: University of California Press, 1997); "Embodiment as a Paradigm for Anthropology," *Ethos* 18, no. 1 (1990): 5:47.
4 Carol M. Worthman, "Emotions: You Can Feel the Difference," in *Biocultural Approaches to the Emotions*, ed. Alexander Laban Hinton, 41–74 (Cambridge: Cambridge University Press, 1999).
5 Rebecca Seligman, ""Bio-Looping" and the Psychophysiological in Religious Belief and Practice: Mechanisms of Embodiment in Candomblé Trance and Possession," in *The Palgrave Handbook of Biology and Society*, eds. Maurizio Meloni, John Cromby, Des Fitzgerald, Stephanie Lloyd, 417–439 (London: Palgrave Macmillan, 2018).
6 *Possessing Spirits and Healing Selves: Embodiment and Transformation in an Afro-Brazilian Religion* (Springer, 2014).
7 Eugene G. d'Aquili and Andrew B. Newberg, "Religious and Mystical States: A Neuropsychological Model," *Zygon* 28, no. 2 (1993): 177–200; Dennis R. Wier, *Trance: From Magic to Technology* (Ann Arbor, MI: Trans Media, 1996).
8 Edward J. Frischholz, Warren W. Tryon, Athena T. Vellios, Stanley Fisher, Brian L. Maruffi, Herbert Spiegel, "The Relationship between the Hypnotic Induction Profile and the Stanford Hypnotic Susceptibility Scale, Form C: A Replication," *American Journal of Clinical Hypnosis* 22, no. 4 (1980): 185–196.
9 Wier, *Trance: From Magic to Technology*; Seligman, *Possessing Spirits and Healing Selves: Embodiment and Transformation in an Afro-Brazilian Religion*; Rebecca Seligman and Laurence J. Kirmayer, "Dissociative Experience and Cultural Neuroscience: Narrative, Metaphor and Mechanism," *Culture, Medicine and Psychiatry* 32, no. 1 (2008): 31–64.

10 Charles Laughlin, John McManus, and Eugene d'Aquili, *The Spectrum of Ritual* (Columbia University Press, 1979); Charles D. Laughlin and Eugene G. d'Aquili, *Biogenetic Structuralism* (Columbia University Press, 1974).

11 Eugene G. d'Aquili and Andrew B. Newberg, *The Mystical Mind* (Minneapolis, MN: Fortress Press, 1999); "Religious and Mystical States: A Neuropsychological Model."

12 "Religious and Mystical States: A Neuropsychological Model."

13 d'Aquili's obituary mentions the inaccessibility of much of his prose.

14 d'Aquili and Newberg, *The Mystical Mind*.

15 Andrew B. Newberg et al., "The Measurement of Regional Cerebral Blood Flow during Glossolalia: A Preliminary SPECT Study," *Psychiatry Research: Neuroimaging* 148, no. 1 (2006): 113–122.

16 Andrew B. Newberg and Bruce Y. Lee, "The Relationship between Religion and Health," in *Where God and Science Meet: How Brain and Evolutionary Studies Alter Our Understanding of Religion*, ed. Patrick McNamara, Psychology, Religion, and Spirituality, 51–81 (Westport, CT: Praeger, 2006).

17 Mihaly Csikszentmihalyi, *Flow: The Psychology of Optimal Experience* (New York: Harper & Row, 1990); Susan A. Jackson and Mihaly Csikszentmihalyi, *Flow in Sports* (Human Kinetics, 1999).

18 Francis Crick and Christof Koch, "A Framework for Consciousness," *Nature Neuroscience* 6, no. 2 (2003): 119–126.

19 Charles J. Limb and Allen R. Braun, "Neural Substrates of Spontaneous Musical Performance: An FMRI Study of Jazz Improvisation," *PLoS One* 3, no. 2 (2008): e1679.

20 Rob Ruck, *The Tropic of Football: The Long and Perilous Journey of Samoans in the NFL* (New York: New Press, 2018).

21 Saturday Down South, "Tua Tagovailoa Reveals He Was 'Really Close' to Transferring from Alabama," *Saturday Down South* (2019), https://www.saturdaydownsouth. com/alabama-football/tua-tagovailoa-says-he-was-really-close-to-transferring-from-alabama/.

22 Bradd Shore, *Sala'ilua-a Samoan Mystery* (New York: Columbia University Press, 1982).

23 Gilbert Rouget, *Music and Trance: A Theory of the Relations between Music and Possession* (Chicago: University of Chicago Press, 1985).

24 E. Rossi, *The Collected Works of Milton H. Erickson, Md (16 Volumes)* (Phoenix: The Milton H. Erickson Foundation Press, 2008).

9

INCENTIVE SALIENCE OF DRINKING AND DRUGGING

Binge Drinking and Blacking Out

Binge drinking is one of the most common and obvious forms of dissociation for young adults. I never liked the taste of alcohol, but in my 20s, I fooled many people. My high school best friend, Brent, started drinking at a young age; and most of the men in my family were drinkers, so I was environmentally predisposed to it as well. Yet I studiously avoided it until, around 15, I decided to find out what I was missing. The first time I drank, I had no idea how much it would take to achieve my objective of becoming inebriated, so I poured it down my throat like water. The setting was like a suburban coming-of-age movie; Brent's parents were out of town, so he was throwing a little party. We had a bottle rocket war that night in the field behind Brent's house using Wiffle® bats with holes in the end or broken golf clubs as handles. By inserting the bottle rocket in the hole at the end, we could hold it away from our bodies and have some control over direction—though not much—as they whirred off into the ground or air and quickly exploded. I managed to shoot Brent in the chest with one, which exploded as it hit him. He was fine, though his pride was hurt and his shirt singed.

Aside from that, I recall little from the evening. Apparently I rode along on a liquor store run with a friend who had a fake ID and mooned people in other cars from the back window as we drove there. My memory is based on what I was told. According to what became lore among my friends, on that night of my first blackout, I had to be repeatedly steered away from the hot tub, walked through a screen door, and embarrassed myself visiting neighbor girls. I had ridden my bike to Brent's house, but I could barely stand the next day after sleeping over, so my parents had to be called to come retrieve me. I was subsequently grounded for about two months for lying to them that Brent's parents would be home during the party.

DOI: 10.4324/9781003034483-9

Blackout drinking experiences, especially the type termed "en bloc" (as opposed to the more common "fragmentary" blackout) are gone from memory, never to be recovered. En bloc blackouts do not come back as fragments, under hypnosis, in dreams, or through years of psychotherapy. Neurologically, they are not even memories. Alcohol progressively impairs the ability to form new memories in a dose-response manner—the more alcohol a person consumes, even starting with just one or two drinks, the greater the impairment of memory formation. After experiencing blackouts many times, I began to monitor myself. I remember thinking while drinking, "I know what's going on. I don't feel so drunk that I won't remember this." And that's the last thing I would remember.[1]

Inebriation does not necessarily prevent short-term memory formation—people may be able to recall information just learned and things stored in long-term memory—but it prevents new long-term memory formation during the period of drunkenness. Whatever was learned and recalled during intoxication is not retained. Scholars who conducted some of the early studies of alcoholism by interviewing alcoholics suggested that state-dependent memory formation occurs during black-outs—in other words, that one has to be blackout drunk again to remember what one did in other blackouts.[2] However, the mechanisms of alcohol-induced memory suppression are now better understood and state-dependent memory formation has been disproven. In rat models, alcohol suppresses activity in CA1 pyramidal cells in the brain's hippocampus. Pyramidal cells are neurons with multiple poles or connection sites, giving them a pyramid-like shape. CA1 refers to the region of the hippocampus where they occur, with CA standing for *cornu Ammon* (Latin for Ammon's horn because of the shape of the hippocampus). CA1 cells are associated with the formation of memories of facts and events. Alcohol also disrupts long-term potentiation, or the ability of neuronal cells to form long-term communication with other nerve cells.[3]

Incentive Salience and Coming of Age

After getting smashed on my first go-round, I felt so physically awful and embarrassed that I swore off drinking in favor of smoking weed, but that changed several years later when I got to college and had another opportunity to drink alcohol. Having learned nothing from my high school binge experience, I held my breath and downed a liter cup of cheap vodka screwdriver. I awakened with vomit *under* my pillow and all over my stylish vintage maroon suede jacket and more gaps in my memory. This experience also taught me nothing, and I carried on drinking to excess. If I never liked the taste of alcohol, why did I drink? I had spent my whole childhood and young adulthood thinking, analyzing possibilities, failing to act, regretting what I had not done. While drunk, I found myself able to do crazy things that made me feel interesting, like I was living a life worth writing about. I was talkative at parties and not worried about saying dumb things. In fact, I became downright exhibitionistic. I was unafraid of talking to girls who interested me and found myself dancing and flirting and even falling into bed with some of them.

My college campus binge drinking experience is not unique, of course. At the University of Alabama, college students regularly stumble into local downtown homes in blackout states, mistakenly thinking they are at friends' or their own homes. Neighbors share anecdotes that range from the mildly annoying to the hilarious or tragic. On the funny end of the spectrum is the naked student who passed out on my friend's porch in downtown Tuscaloosa. When the police showed up, poked him awake, and asked what he was doing, he replied, "Duh! Sleeping!" On the nearly tragic side is the girl who went through a glass door and would have bled out, but the homeowners' alarm and cameras alerted them of an intruder and the video feed that went to an app on their phone showed that she was bleeding heavily. One story goes back to the early days of the University of Alabama, in around 1830, when a resident of what is now the wealthy historic neighborhood in the heart of the student drinking district threatened to shoot the next student who stumbled drunkenly across his property. And then he did—in the leg, not fatally—and felt so bad that he built a new mansion farther away from the University. As Kevin Stroud relates on his *History of English* podcast, the founding of universities is linked to binge drinking. In the early days of what would become Oxford University, the second oldest university in Europe, founded in 1096, the congregation of young drunk out-of-town students was so rowdy that locals hanged several in revenge for a death blamed on one of them. This prompted the teachers and students to move a safe distance away to Cambridge and ultimately found the university there.[4]

The incentives and rewards surrounding the use of drugs are as powerful and as synergistic in addiction as the drug actions themselves. In other words, the process of craving, obtaining, and preparing to use substances is as addictive as the physiological action they exert, precisely because it is highly rewarding to the brain. This is particularly true when the pleasure of use is no longer powerful. Incentive salience, "works in conjunction with learning, pleasure, habit, and other neural dynamics that shape behavior."[5] In this light, my drinking was not just a response to peer pressure or a desire to conform to social norms. It was much more meaningful. It was tied to growing up, and it emerged at a particular developmental stage when I was learning how to be social, how to achieve my biological imperative of reproductive fitness, and pruning my dendritic connections in concert with these ends. Now, as a father, husband, and teacher with nearly two decades of relative sobriety behind me, this context of use and abuse has little appeal, but I remember those feelings poignantly. It gives me, as we say in my house, "backward feelings" or dread at the thought of repeating those experiences. My brain still feels like it is constantly and exhaustingly on, and the desire to dissociate from that persistent anxious mentation was one thing that led me to drink in the first place. But as I've gotten older, I've learned to seek different and mostly healthier ways to balance my life, to get my mind to rest when I don't want it scouting ahead to spot all the potential stressors of the day or week or month.

In the meantime, beginning my freshman year of college, I quickly slipped into what drug researchers called the "joints" subculture among marijuana users. A joint is a hand-rolled marijuana cigarette using the rolling papers that come with loose leaf smoking tobacco or that can be purchased separately anywhere tobacco products are sold. A joints subculture refers to illicit marijuana use in social settings among people also characterized by the way they use the drug, as well as inter-related constellations of music, clothing, slang, and tattoo style preferences, for example.[6] Researchers from the National Development and Research Institutes who have collected data on drug use and markets have outlined certain elements of these drug subcultures to be more distinctive for empirical research purposes, though in reality there are high degrees of overlap.[7]

Smoking weed via joints, pipes, and bongs (water pipes) became the focus of social behavior for my college friends and I during this period. We spent a lot of money and credit and went to considerable and sometimes dangerous lengths to acquire the substance we preferred for altering our consciousness. I would find myself in the homes of people I barely knew or sketchy people I'd just met. If we couldn't score on campus, we would drive every week or two to a guy we knew who lived out in the country, which took around an hour. During the few years I was buying from him, this guy lived on his parents' farm, in a house with his grandmother and pregnant wife and later their infant. His wife used to have him help her get high from a 5-foot long bong to curb her pregnancy sickness. After their kid was born, they moved upstairs in the same farmhouse, where he set up a grow room in a large walk-in closet to raise his own marijuana plants in secret and left the downstairs to his grandmother, who was disabled and could not climb the stairs. We would be smoking upstairs, and his grandmother would be downstairs yelling up at him. He would scream at her as my college buddies and I sat there glancing uncomfortably at each other. We'd often have to hang out at his house while this guy drove somewhere to score for all of us if he didn't have weed for sale on hand. His grandmother would yell up the stairs while he was gone, and we'd get nervous and pretend we weren't there, whispering to each other. Then we'd drive back to campus stoned out of our minds, trying to stay focused on the road in the dark.

I followed my high school buddy Brent and moved to New York City when I was 21. Buying weed there was a lot different. At first, I had no connections. I would either score via Brent and his Bronx friends in upstate New York or on the street in Washington Square Park. "Rastas" would be at the gates of the park, where they'd whisper, "Psst. Psst. Weed." We called them "Rastas" because they were generally men with Caribbean accents and dreadlocks dressed in the typical Rastafarian colors of yellow, green, and red. I would nod to them, and then sit on a bench. They'd come sit next to me. We would both look up and around to see if anyone was watching and negotiate the exchange without actually looking at each other. I'd slip them a ten-dollar bill for a dime-bag. They'd go to another person in the park, or to a tree, planter, or nearby stoop where they had their drug stash concealed so if they got arrested nothing would be found on their person, then come back with my weed.

A five-year "Marijuana/Blunts: Use, Subcultures and Markets" study of "retail" marijuana purchasing from that period supports my experience and suggests that I was moving from the more traditional joints subculture of my suburban roots to the blunts subculture of urban NYC.[8] The chief distinction worth noting here is that hand-rolling marijuana to smoke using cigarette papers is an older form of consumption prevalent among most marijuana users until the 1980s. Blunts are essentially marijuana rolled in the tobacco leaves used to roll cigars instead of cigarette papers, a practice that likely developed in Jamaica because cigarette papers were harder to come by or because the tobacco smell masked the marijuana odor or for both reasons. Blunts are much larger than joints, and the addition of tobacco contributes another sensation to the euphoria produced by marijuana. This consumption preference traveled with Caribbean migrants to US urban centers like New York City. The term "blunt" derives from a habit of using the Phillies Blunt™ brand of cigar that was cheap and widely available in any corner store.[9]

Prices and quality varied between downtown, around Washington Square in Greenwich Village and Tompkins Square on the Lower East Side, where the buyers were ethnically diverse but included many White ones, and uptown in the Bronx and Harlem, where buyers were primarily Black and Hispanic. The stuff I was scoring off the street was lower grade "commercial" weed. The period from 1975 to 1995 in New York City was marked by limited enforcement of small-scale marijuana trafficking and use. Street-level sales boomed and became commonplace, such that even non-users were accustomed to the aggressiveness of sellers in parks like Washington Square; and, according to these researchers, West Indian immigrants *claiming* to be Rastafari were particularly effective at importing marijuana from the West Indies for sale in NYC.[10]

Right around the time of my arrival in NYC, things started to shift. Street-level marijuana sales and use and open alcohol containers were practically ignored by police when I visited Brent at college, and in my first few months living in NYC. But many sellers traded in crack, cocaine, and heroin as well marijuana. The crime associated with these narcotics was more threatening, as drug crews took to controlling whole city blocks and undermined the security of local residents. For instance, we scored coke in the first few months after my arrival on the street a block from the famous punk club CBGB on the Bowery, where we had gone to see some bands, and on Ludlow Street near Max Fish, another regular haunt. But I arrived just before the incumbent David Dinkins—New York City's first African-American mayor—was defeated by Republican Rudolph Giuliani, who promised to take back the streets and improve municipal quality of life. Giuliani became notorious for these efforts and the "zero tolerance" policies of the era, which extended from increased enforcement of street-level surveillance of drug sales and drug and alcohol use to banning of street vending of anything in some areas, including food and art in tourist areas.[11]

Weed storefronts—the second mode of retail in NYC's Lower East Side—were more reliable for people who had access. The storefronts were dependent on repeat customers and staffed by familiar faces, so the chances of getting ripped off were lower.[12] I was vouchsafed by friends from Brooklyn and got membership cards to at least three different weed stores. The first was a Rasta store on 3rd Street across from the Hells Angels clubhouse. They sold reggae music, incense, and Rastafarian merchandise as their cover. To buy weed, you needed a membership card. I'd ring the buzzer outside to be let into the store, show the card at the front desk, then proceed to the back of the store. There I would put money in a drawer that came out of the wall where my money would be replaced by a bag of weed. Then I had to buy something from the storefront, so if police were watching, it would be less obvious it was a weed spot. I bought a lot of incense.

Later on, I was dating a girl whose roommate was a weed dealer who delivered via bike—the third mode of retail going on at that time in the LES.[13] The weed connection outlasted the romance. He would only deliver in Manhattan, and I lived in Queens, so I'd call him from work, and he'd come right to my office. Bike and foot weed delivery was common in NYC at that time. The weed was generally higher-grade "designer" varieties that cost much more than what was available in stores or the street. As messengers for legitimate businesses are ubiquitous in NYC, policing weed messengers was nearly impossible. Most maintained small, exclusive client lists to remain inconspicuous.[14]

In the US, alcohol and, increasingly, marijuana and other drugs are so integral to culture and economics that wars are waged over their use and distribution. My coming-of-age decade, the 1980s, was dominated by President Reagan's "War on Drugs." Ironically, the '80s are noted for the crack epidemic. In the early '90s, the US illicit drug subcultures transitioned to an emphasis on weed. A shift toward legalization in the last decade has changed the landscape tremendously. At the time of this writing, medical and recreational marijuana legalization are on the rise in the US.

Did We Co-Evolve with the Plants That Alter Us?

Several scholars have made cases for a co-evolution between humans and the substances we use to achieve dissociative states. Biologist Robert Dudley suggests that primates may have a predisposition toward imbibing alcohol, for instance. Among primates most closely related to humans are chimpanzees, whose diets consist of over 85% ripe fruit. They spend much of their foraging time seeking ripe fruit and choosing particular pieces. Most primates live in tropical regions of the world, where yeasts that produce alcohol on fruit also thrive at a higher rate than in cooler areas. Like other organisms that utilize ripe fruit, primates may use the smell of alcohol as a means of detecting it. Female fruit flies rely on the smell of alcohol to locate fruit on which to lay their eggs. The alcohol intake of contemporary non-human primates and our ancestors has probably generally been at low levels but may have had a significant enough impact to provide an advantage for those better able to detect and seek it out. This motivation has had the same impact as the selected-for trait to seek out sugar and salt, sources of which were rare in our ancestral environment but which can now be easily mass-produced on the cheap.[15]

Dudley outlines how fruit interacts with yeast to produce alcohol naturally. Unripe fruit is full of tannins to ward off creatures that might eat it before the seed is mature. However, when the seed is ready to be proliferated, the tannins dissipate from the meat of the fruit and more sugars are produced. The sugar is the fuel of yeast, which colonizes the fruit and produces alcohol as a weapon to ward off other bacteria from getting the sugar. Yeast and bacteria are not the only creatures in the neighborhood that like the quick calories of ripe fruit sugar. Primates and many other mammals co-evolved with flowering plants and fruit. Ripe fruit signals to primates that it is ready to be eaten when it changes color, and primates rely to a great extent on color vision. But the smell of ripe fruit is also crucial, so much so that even our less sophisticated human olfaction can readily detect the smell of ripe fruit, especially as it begins to ferment or become overripe.[16]

When a smaller-bodied primate eats ripened fruit, even with a low alcohol content, it has a small psychotropic effect, stimulating more hunger. The primate then eats more fruit and gets a lot of energy in the bargain. It does the fruit a favor by spitting the seeds around or defecating them out elsewhere, and the whole thing serves as a positive feedback loop, encouraging the behavior in a big cycle of win–win. That is, until humans come along and figure out how to mass-produce alcohol.[17]

The trouble with alcohol, notes Dudley, is the same as with potato chips and candy bars (or salt and sugar). We need them at low levels. Research shows that people who drink moderately have better health outcomes than heavy drinkers *or* teetotalers. But some people go bonkers, eat a whole bag of chips in a sitting, gorge on Halloween candy, or drink to intoxication. Archaeologist Patrick "Dr. Pat" McGovern goes further. He notes that the galaxy has clouds of alcohol, which suggests these substances play a role in the molecular fabric of being. Dr. Pat has traced the history and prehistory of alcohol consumption in antiquity and has notably recreated ancient alcoholic beverages using chemical residues found in ancient pottery. It turns out our ancestors were way ahead of us in the boutique microbrewing trend, developing beers and wines containing all manner of fruits, spices, and flavors.[18]

We may have coevolved with flowering plants to be attracted to the alcoholic by-product of their fruits' fermentation, but what about weed? Journalist Michael Pollan suggests that humans are not necessarily the genius domesticators of plants and animals we tend to credit ourselves as. If the unconscious goal of a gene is to get itself reproduced, then the genes in domesticated species are the masters of the universe. However, reproduction is really based on the preferential selection of phenotypes, not just a few genes clamoring to be passed on to the next animal or plant offspring. Certain phenotypes are broadly seductive. As Pollan outlines, this is as true of cannabis as it is of apples, tulips, and potatoes. The ancestors of these domesticates stumbled onto human motivations as means to flourish, and, consequently, we have carried them around the globe, planted them everywhere, and protected their production with machetes, guns, and lives.[19]

Cannabis rose from a weedy little plant from Kazakhstan to become a highly sought-after cash crop around the world. Like its friends the poppy and coca plant, wars are fought to grow and protect these plants. Like all exogenous substances, several of the chemicals in cannabis react with endogenous neurotransmitters in humans. This is not to say that we evolved to smoke weed, but all drugs that we use or take, including caffeine, interact with our natural neurotransmitters. They either act as agonists, facilitating the same activity as endogenous substances evolved for those neurotransmitters, or as antagonists, reversing or blocking the neurotransmitter activity. And some of those agonists are superfacilitators, amping up the facilitation. This is a simplistic explanation because many of these interactions have more sophisticated regulatory effects in concert with endogenous chemistry, but the gist is that pot co-opts neurotransmitters in the human body to produce a feeling commonly described as being "high." This highness involves serotonergic and dopaminergic systems, which moderate mood and pleasure, resulting in a positive feedback motivation to experience it again. This motivation to re-experience the feeling of being high entices humans to plant and protect cannabis.

Humans have found ways other than the abuse of alcohol or recreational drugs to get in our own way and blind ourselves to reality. In the penultimate chapter, I address another common type of dissociation that appears to be adaptive in its normal and largely invisible manifestation but can really screw up the world when it is operating at a societal level.

Notes

1 Donald W. Goodwin, J. Bruce Crane, and Samuel B. Guze, "Alcoholic 'Blackouts': A Review and Clinical Study of 100 Alcoholics," *American Journal of Psychiatry* 126, no. 2 (1969): 191–198.
2 Ibid.
3 Aaron M. White, "What Happened? Alcohol, Memory Blackouts, and the Brain," *Alcohol Research and Health* 27, no. 2 (2003): 186–196.
4 Episode 95: "Old School and New School," http://historyofenglishpodcast.com/2017/06/15/episode-95-old-school-and-new-school/.
5 Daniel H. Lende, "Addiction and Neuroanthropology," in *The Encultured Brain: An Introduction to Neuroanthropology*, eds. Daniel H. Lende and Greg Downey, 339–362 (Cambridge, MA: MIT Press, 2012); Terry E. Robinson and Kent C. Berridge, "Incentive-Sensitization and Addiction," *Addiction* 96, no. 1 (2001): 103–114.
6 Geoffrey L. Ream et al., "Distinguishing Blunts Users from Joints Users: A Comparison of Marijuana Use Subcultures," in *New Research on Street Drugs*, ed. Spencer M. Cole, 245–273 (New York: Nova Science Publishers, 2006).
7 Andrew Golub, Bruce D. Johnson, and Eloise Dunlap, "Subcultural Evolution and Illicit Drug Use," *Addiction Research & Theory* 13, no. 3 (2005): 217–229.
8 Ream et al., "Distinguishing Blunts Users from Joints Users: A Comparison of Marijuana Use Subcultures."
9 Caitlyn Hitt, "The Tightly-Rolled History of the Blunt," https://www.thrillist.com/news/nation/what-is-a-blunt-history-origins-timeline.
10 B.D. Johnson et al., "Policing and Social Control of Public Marijuana Use and Selling in New York City," *Law Enforcement Executive Forum* 6, no. 5 (2006): 59–89; Stephen J. Sifaneck et al., "Retail Marijuana Purchases in Designer and Commercial Markets in New York City: Sales Units, Weights, and Prices Per Gram," *Drug and Alcohol Dependence* 90, no. Supplement 1 (2007): S40–S51.
11 Johnson et al., "Policing and Social Control of Public Marijuana Use and Selling in New York City."
12 Sifaneck et al., "Retail Marijuana Purchases in Designer and Commercial Markets in New York City: Sales Units, Weights, and Prices Per Gram."
13 Ibid.

14 Ibid.
15 Robert Dudley, *The Drunken Monkey: Why We Drink and Abuse Alcohol* (Berkeley, CA: University of California Press, 2014).
16 Ibid.
17 Ibid.
18 Patrick E. McGovern, *Uncorking the Past: The Quest for Wine, Beer, and Other Alcoholic Beverages* (Berkeley, CA: University of California Press, 2009).
19 Michael Pollan, *The Botany of Desire: A Plant's-Eye View of the World* (Random House Trade Paperbacks, 2001).

10

ADAPTIVE AND MALADAPTIVE AT THE SAME TIME

The Fine Arts of Deception and Manipulation

Manipulation is not unique to humans. The East African insect *Acanthaspis petax* (a type of assassin bug) disguises itself with the bodies of dead ants to confuse predators and sneak into ant colonies to feast on its inhabitants. Among mixed-species flocks of birds in the Amazon rainforest, antshrikes often forage on open ground at the center of the flock and fake danger calls if they spot an insect they want for themselves. Baboons will sometimes induce dominant troupe members to attack a third conspecific by feigning grievance. This social skill is mastered by baboons at puberty, though they may not develop skill with physical tools, like using stones to crack hard nuts, until they are adults. Primates appear naturally disposed to manipulate social tools with more ease and sophistication than physical ones.[1]

Manipulation and deception have been noticed among all families of monkeys and apes, wherein these abilities serve to affect others' attention—distracting them, misdirecting them, etc.—but seem to be primarily learned situational tactics rather than deliberately planned strategies of behavior.[2] However, even imitating such behavior without insight about motives remains a great leap forward in the efficiency of learning because these shortcuts reduce the inherent dangers of trial and error.[3] Mixing and matching behaviors from different people into our own style and behavioral repertoire, a process called "idea foraging," is something humans do with a great deal of subtlety.[4]

This subtlety lends itself to deception, a behavior with obvious benefits. Dependence on a social group comprising members of all ages, with conflicting needs and desires, necessarily leads to manipulation. Yet, in maintaining the balance of group living, self-serving manipulation that disrupts the group may be more costly than beneficial, so balance needs to be achieved. In particular, manipulation would be favored in which the manipulated is unaware of being manipulated or of

DOI: 10.4324/9781003034483-10

losing, as with certain types of deceit, or in which there is a compensatory gain, as with some forms of cooperation.[5]

For humans, the problem is the stigma associated with the lie: "honesty" is promoted by the moral codes of most societies, while "dishonesty" is condemned because it makes people less predictable, making social life more treacherous to navigate. Yet the human psyche would not have evolved in a world of truthfulness and sincerity. The complexity of consciousness is a direct outcome of manipulation, and truth itself can be a tool of this game, used when cost-effective. Reputations for truthfulness and honesty become, under such circumstances, so much cultural currency.[6]

Moreover, such manipulations extend to the self, and self-deceptive individuals who seem to look at life through rose-colored glasses often have better health outcomes than pessimists. Depressed persons have more realistic views of themselves than normal people, suggesting that a degree of self-deception is a boon to self-esteem. People who undergo surgery for heart disease but maintain denial about the severity of their condition spend less time in intensive care, have fewer signs of cardiac dysfunction during hospitalization and adjust better for the first few months after surgery than do low deniers.[7] Those who self-deceptively enhance their own qualities are also less psychologically and physiologically stressed about completing novel, complex tasks—i.e., they are not hampered by analysis paralysis. Another study found such high self-deceivers also display greater tolerance of pain and discomfort than people lower in self-deception.[8]

Self-deception may help protect people from mental illness by, in part, reducing cognitive dissonance and stress. People who are adaptively self-enhancing tend to portray things about themselves as more positive than reality merits. This tactic may be used to avoid embarrassment or criticism, preserve optimism, and manage impressions. Self-deception hides narcissistic motivations from the self, that they may be more easily hidden from others. A moderate degree of narcissism is useful for most people to get basic needs met, especially when resources are limited, but in general, it is not socially acceptable to baldly admit self-interest, especially if one's interests conflict with those of others. Instead, the mind goes through complex machinations to avoid self-insight.[9]

Lying to Oneself to Manipulate Others

Compared to studies of the extreme dissociation of shamanic and possession trance practices or the medical study of hypnosis, much less investigation has been conducted cross-culturally on self-deceit as a form of dissociation. "Denial" is what we tend to call self-deception in English-speaking countries. In Amazonia, the same etic is expressed among the Muinane people of Amazonian Colombia as a belief that all plants and animals are human.[10] Most contemporary humans have shifted to the worldview that all *Homo sapiens* are humans based on morphological similarities, and we view other creatures as animals. According to the Muinane, animals see *themselves* as human and other creatures, including us, as the animals. This view is hierarchical, with humans as the wholly good and moral creatures and animals as bad. Therefore, when a human does something deemed bad, that person is said to have been invaded by a particular animal essence, thereby absolving the person of a certain amount of responsibility and guilt.[11]

This Muinane pattern combines both a denial-projection axis typical of self-deception and a possession phenomenon, wherein an invading essence is wholly or partially responsible for actions in the eyes of both the individual and the culture. The Muinane believe that people are possessed by malicious animal spirits; they are not utilizing the belief system as a ploy to avoid personal responsibility. Yet this is essentially the end result.[12] Anthropologist E.E. Evans-Pritchard documented similar behavior among the Azande of North Central Africa.[13] Reluctance to accept personal responsibility or bad luck for misfortune and attribution to witchcraft is also a functional form of denial and projection. Rather than projecting blame onto another person who could deny, or worse, return the accusation, the Azande blame an animal or an unknown person or spirit.

Self-deception is acting in ways contrary to patently clear evidence but is problematically associated with knowing and not knowing. Some scholars suggest it is impossible to deceive oneself—that if one knows something, well, it is known. It can't not be known. However, there are at least three possible ways one can, in fact, know and not know. We can know something and forget. Psychologist Christopher Frost and colleagues provide an example from Camus' *The Fall* in which a lawyer greets people cheerily he has had negative interactions with in court.[14] His reputation is that he is an upstanding person who does not take his work personally, when in fact he merely forgets where he knows these people from and greets them all with good cheer. We can also know something but convince ourselves of the contrary until we believe it. The example of late basketball star Kobe Bryant was used by law professor Andrew Taslitz in reviewing forensic cases of self-deception.[15] Bryant was accused of date rape. When investigators interviewed him, they asked, "Did she say 'no'?" He responded with a deflection and was asked again, upon which he paused, looked away, and responded "no," she did not say no. He seemed to believe this, a claim that could have been tested with skin conductance (lie detector), but the investigators interpreted his answer as deluded honesty. She probably said "no," but the context was such that he truly thought it meant "yes." Since he could not convey the context sufficiently to convince the investigators, he came to the conclusion that she had said "yes" in a manner of speaking and presented himself convincingly in this way. A third form of plausible knowing and not knowing is through a modular mind, or the idea that our brains come with some completely separated neural networks within the same skull that process similar information. Thus, it could be possible to have separate but conflicting information in different parts of the brain that do not, as a matter of course, come into contact with each other. I think of this like conflicting schedules. Sometimes I make two different sets of plans for the same time—say, I schedule a speaker to come to my university and later book myself to attend a workshop out of town on the same date (true story)—but, if I don't write them both down in the same calendar, I fail to think of one thing when I'm talking about the other. Therefore, until the time comes when the separate plans come into direct conflict, I don't realize I've been doing it.

These examples only marginally rise to the level of self-deception, however, according to evolutionary biologist Robert Trivers, who believes that an intention to deceive is a key element of self-deception. Trivers is best known for modeling the concepts of parent-offspring conflict and reciprocal altruism in evolutionary biology, but in the introduction he penned for Richard Dawkins' 1976 classic *The Selfish Gene*, Trivers speculated that conflicts are inherent to biological systems, from genes up to societies.[16] Deception is a natural aspect of conflict, and the interaction between deception in one party, side, organism, etc., and deception-detection on the other leads to an arms race. Each side is pressured to survive by increasing the ability to deceive or detect deception. Ultimately, the only way to carry off deception under such circumstances is to eliminate all detectable traces of deception by not even being aware that one is being deceptive and that self-deception is the "active misrepresentation of reality to the conscious mind."[17]

In 1979, Trivers became friends with Black Panther Party founder Huey P. Newton through a reading course Trivers taught on deception and self-deception. Together, they wrote an article in 1982 after the crash of Air Florida Flight 90 as a poignant example of tragic self-deception. Trivers had been scheduled to do a lecture tour but canceled due to snowstorms blanketing the East Coast, the same snowstorm that brought down Flight 90. Bob Silberglied, a former colleague of Trivers at Harvard who studied deception in insects was on that flight and was not among the survivors. The transcript of the conversation between the pilot and copilot, retrieved from the black box recording after the wreckage was fished from the Potomac River, clearly indicated that the copilot was nervously questioning the pilot about conditions but that the pilot was overconfident until too late. The pilot's overconfidence may have generally served him well in other minor situations but was fatal when the real danger of ice on the plane's wings required him to pay close attention to reality and to the obvious anxiety of his copilot. The benefit of self-deception, say Trivers and Newton, "is the more fluid deception of others. The cost is an impaired ability to deal with reality."[18]

In 2003, I visited Trivers at Rutgers University when I was considering going to grad school there to study self-deception. He gave me an autographed copy of his 2000 update on evolution and self-deception and encouraged my interest, as he had not yet had time to pursue the idea further. I had little idea at that time who Trivers was in the field of evolutionary biology or that *Time* Magazine had named him as one of the 100 greatest thinkers and scientists of the 20th century and thought it was strange that a professor would autograph a paper. I laugh looking at it now with the notes that I scribbled all over it. In that 2000 paper, Trivers wrote again about Flight 90, which didn't mean much to me at the time. However, he had added analysis of the Space Shuttle Challenger disaster, which I saw blow up shortly after launch, live on national television, when my high school freshman English teacher let us watch Sally Ride go into space.

The Space Shuttle Challenger disaster, caused by faulty O-ring safety gaskets, is an example of organizational self-deception. NASA had set a goal in the 1960s of putting a man on the moon before the Soviets. Once this was accomplished, NASA had a bloated bureaucracy with a huge budget that needed to be continually justified lest all those people lose their high-paying, prestigious government jobs. The public goals of the Space Shuttle program therefore were to develop a reusable spacecraft that could send more people into space and to maintain the international prestige of the US space program. Choices were made more to retain NASA's large budget than because of mission logic. For instance, manned flights were preferred to unmanned flights because the former cost more. Likewise, the reusable space shuttles were more expensive to maintain than using new vehicles each time.[19]

The O-rings that sealed the rocket boosters to prevent explosions on takeoff were designed from the top-down, based on cost, rather than from a bottom-up eye on safety. To understand this, Trivers points to elevator safety protocols. Cables holding elevators are said to be safe if they can move the elevators with absolutely zero damage to the cable, then they increase the strength of the cable by a factor of 11. They call this an 11-fold safety factor. Seven of 24 space shuttle flights before Challenger had exhibited O-ring damage. In one case, one-third of the ring disintegrated, and the shuttle would have blown up if it had disintegrated completely. NASA stated that the 2/3 remaining was a sign of the strength of the O-ring, calling their approach a three-fold safety factor.[20]

One way of understanding this phenomenon is that the unconscious mind is actively misrepresenting something to the conscious mind without resorting to Ancient Greek beliefs in homunculi in our heads running the show. However, this sets up an unrealistic binary; there is no one absolute conscious mind and no one absolute unconscious mind.[21] As I hope I've made clear so far, the mind is different degrees of awareness. The real question is, when there are so many negative examples of maladaptive self-deception, why hasn't it been purged from our species through processes of natural selection?

The conclusion Trivers reaches is that self-deception must be adaptive at the unit of selection—in mating or agonistic (i.e., combative) encounters. In mating scenarios—which is the context of selection and reproductive fitness or the coin of the evolutionary realm—males and females are essentially competing.[22] A simplified model of this sexual strategy (called Bateman's Principle) is that females have a limited number of valuable ovum and need resources. Males have an unlimited supply of highly expendable sperm and need eggs. Trivers' "parental investment theory" revises this model, suggesting that the sex that puts more resources into parenting exerts the most influence on selection of traits in the other sex. Usually this is females, but in some species, it is males. Thus, males (usually) need to convince females that they have resources and are willing to share.[23]

The burden of proof in this sexual competition is generally on the males, so we already see a motivation for deception. According to error management theory, human females err to the side of skepticism of male intentions and are generally on the lookout for dishonesty. Females elicit indications of male resources or capacities to acquire resources (including intelligence but also occupations, status, and other wealth indicators) through some hard-to-fake or costly signals of ability. An example of costly displays of ability among non-humans is the rutting behavior of red deer, who spar with each other and lock antlers to vie for the role of protector of females and their offspring. Males with larger antlers are at an advantage in this competition and therefore more likely to be selected. Large antlers do not guarantee protection of resources, but they suggest said deer is *more likely* to be successful than stags with smaller antlers. Thus, large antlers are a sign of potential underlying fitness that is impossible for stags to fake.[24] When I was in graduate school, one of my peers conducted a study to see if engagement rings serve a similar purpose in humans. The idea behind the study was that an expensive ring from a male suitor tells a woman that there is more where that came from and he'll be able to provide for a family, a prediction that was generally supported.[25] It is hard and probably very foolish to fake being wealthy by purchasing an expensive ring (customarily equivalent to one year's salary) to give away. One should be ready to commit to the relationship at that price, which is the idea, but of course some people think they're in love or ready for marriage and are not.

Some people are more self-aware than others and tend to overplay their hands. However, there are those who also fail to toot their own horns and sell themselves short as a result. As I discussed in previous chapters, among the costs of self-awareness is analysis paralysis. An overweening sense of self-awareness may actually undermine confidence in mating scenarios. In an experimental study I conducted with colleagues Nate Pipitone and Julian Keenan, we tested the benefits of self-deception with regard to four simple categories of potential mating success. Individuals can be, at one end of this continuum, low in self-awareness and high in self-deceptive enhancement or, at the other end, high in self-awareness and low in self-deceptive enhancement. We measured reproductive success in males by asking all participants the number of opposite sex sexual partners an individual has had. For males, this represents the number of individuals that he could have potentially impregnated. We measured reproductive success in females in terms of socioeconomic status of her partner, her partner's parents, and her partner's GPA (grade point average). This approximated her ability to garner resources through mate selection.[26]

No studies like this had ever been conducted to my knowledge because self-deception is notoriously difficult to measure, especially relevant to such a distant outcome like reproductive success. We used the questionnaire about self-deception I mentioned in Chapter 6 called the Balanced Inventory of Desirable Responding (BIDR), which includes subscales that measure self-deceptive enhancement and impression management, and another self-deception metric called the Overclaiming Questionnaire. The BIDR measures straightforward self-deceptive enhancement and impression management, which don't necessarily relate to reproductive success.[27] Consequently, the link between self-deception measured by the BIDR and reproductive success for males or females was weak. The Overclaiming Questionnaire, on the other hand, asks people to indicate which items in a list of things likely to be familiar they are in fact familiar with. In each list are a couple "foils," or fake items that appear to belong but don't.[28]

We primed participants by suggesting that people with more cultural knowledge tend to have more sex partners, and people who claim to be familiar with fake items are likely to have overclaimed their knowledge of real items as well. And indeed, while teasing out "reproductive fitness" from a questionnaire study that queries the number of sex partners among a college student sample cannot actually be generalized to say much about evolution, it is a start. People who overclaimed more tended to have had more sex partners, and that association was statistically significant.[29]

Societal Implications of Self-Deception

The most obvious case of self-deception is one I've avoided until now because it's almost too obvious to merit discussion. From at least 2011 until his election in 2016, Donald Trump was the most prominent proponent of the "birther" conspiracy, a false claim that President Obama was not born in the US. This assertion was repeated in the face of easy-to-find evidence to the contrary. Despite the seeming absurdity of using something easily disproved as a political wedge, it works. Even after President Obama produced his US birth certificate, Trump's anti-Obama propaganda continued. Was that self-deception? It's difficult to believe Trump actually believed what he was saying, but it is clear that many American voters wanted to believe it and deceived themselves despite contrary evidence. Likewise, from the 1980s to now, as Trump claimed to be a great deal broker, touting as much in his bestselling *Art of the Deal*, when in fact his businesses have largely been failures.[30]

Trump's true area of expertise, it turns out, is the manipulation of public sentiment to accumulate power. Trivers points out that the adaptive benefits of self-deception are to give one an edge, and in that respect, Trump epitomizes success. He has wielded self-deception as a blunt cudgel, with surprising effectiveness. Despite his claims of fantastic wealth, Trump's objective does not seem to have been the collection of giant piles of gold and jewels to roost upon like Smaug, the dragon from *The Hobbit*. Instead, the manipulation of wealth and facts have been used to cloak himself in the trappings of prosperity and all that becoming rich signals to others. He has used his image as a self-made business maverick who is outside the boundaries of middle-class propriety to portray himself as an average guy, as when he bragged to *Access Hollywood* anchor Billy Bush about grabbing women by the pussy on camera. Before and after, in either glaring self-deception or bold lying, he has stated how much he respects women.[31]

One of Trump's main tactics in interaction with adversaries is the denial-projection axis mentioned previously. Denial and projection are basic psychological processes that abet self-deception. For example, there is as much or more evidence of Trump's false claims than there is of Hillary Clinton's, his Democratic adversary in the 2016 election, yet he labeled her "Crooked Hillary" to deflect away from his own troubles. He has mocked Democratic adversary Joe Biden for his age and refers to him as

"Sleepy Joe" despite only being separated by three years in age. He called North Korean leader Kim Jong-un "Little Rocket Man" though it is Trump who called for establishing a new branch of the military in outer space (despite already having a military branch in charge of space—the US Air Force). The list of these denials and projections goes on, as most contemporary readers of this chapter will know.[32]

Trump's ascendancy to the US presidency exemplifies adaptive self-deception, if placing one's children and in-laws in positions of power can be supposed to enhance reproductive success. While unquestionably beneficial to his own family, this character trait was cataclysmic as a means of running a country. Trivers suggests at least five examples in which self-deception can flourish—denial of ongoing deception, unconscious modules involving deception, self-deception as self-promotion, construction of biased social theory, and fictitious narratives of intention—all of which Trump has illustrated in spades.

Trump's denial of Russian manipulation of the 2016 US election in his own favor and against Hillary Clinton is refuted by piles of evidence substantiating those activities, to say nothing of the longer-term deception Trump and other financiers perpetrated to try to eliminate trade sanctions against Russia. Rachel Maddow's book *Blowout* documents the shell game Trump and his colleagues engaged in with Vladimir Putin and the role Rex Tillerson of Exxon Oil played in the ongoing deception to exploit Russian oil reserves. Trump's naming of Tillerson as Secretary of State was a move toward getting sanctions that have stymied Russian commerce removed. The underlying financial objective by those involved in that international debacle, since well before Trump's rise to the presidency, had been to make US business interests rich and, from Putin's perspective, to make *Russia* great again.[33]

Trivers points to his own unconscious theft of pens, markers, and lighters from the offices of colleagues as a predisposition for self-deception that seems modularly isolated in his brain from his consciousness. Trivers takes these things while talking to colleagues but is not aware he is doing it until he later finds them in his pockets.[34] It's not clear how widespread such idiosyncratic behavior is, but Trump resemble Trivers in this trait. For instance, since well before his election, Trump's trumpeting of unvetted claims and name-calling of opposition via Twitter have made even fellow Republicans comment that this behavior is unbecoming of a president. Yet, even as it became well-established fact that wearing facemasks lowers the transmission risk of COVID-19, Trump steadfastly refused to model such behavior, claiming it made him look "weak" and "unpresidential." Like Trivers, he seems to have a modularly isolated segment of his mind that considers one behavior unpresidential while exhibiting another unpresidential behavior on Twitter. Moreover, Trump deceives himself in promoting the accomplishments of his administration. While bragging that they were doing a great job addressing the COVID-19 pandemic, the US had the highest number of COVID-19 cases and COVID-19-related deaths of any country in the world, with infection rates continuing to climb while those of most other countries were starting to drop. The US was doing such a "good" job that Europe banned travelers from the US from entering the EU.[35]

Many of the social theories about the world works and the role of the US on the global stage were biased and self-serving. Trump has misinterpreted theories about who comes to the United States and why to achieve his own ends, which suggests that he is deceiving himself about his stance on immigration. For instance, though his mother, grandfather, first wife, and current wife all came to the US as immigrants, Trump glommed onto populist fears of Muslims and other immigrants and ran on an anti-immigration platform, vowing to build a wall between the US and Mexico and make the Mexican government pay for it. And Trump consistently seems to make up stories to try to make sense of his intentions after the fact. In June 2020, Trump retweeted a video taken at a protest at a retirement community in Florida where a man driving a golf cart with "Trump 2020" and "America First" signs on it can be heard shouting "White power," but Trump claimed not to have heard the shouting. He also claimed that he does not support White power, despite having called White power advocates who marched in Charlottesville, Virginia, in 2018 "very good people." Also in June 2020, Trump gave a speech inside the White House garden about how he supported peaceful protestors while nearby flashbang grenades were being used by US military personnel to break up a peaceful protest on Trump's order. Trump wanted the way clear to walk from the White House to St. John's Episcopal Church across the street after his speech and hold up a bible for a photo shoot.[36]

In some ways, politicians have to be more dissociative and self-deceptive than other people because they are constant targets of criticism and disapproval. I hated admiring 43rd US president George W. Bush for his seemingly jovial indifference to the disapproval registered by a good half or more of the American people during his terms in office. It would be difficult to withstand constant criticism without sturdy psychological defense mechanisms. My kids noted how fascinating it was to live through these times and be witness to the constant turmoil churned up by the 45th Commander-in-Chief. As Adam Gaffney of *The Guardian* says, if Hollywood portrayed a US president who ruled by self-deception, it would have to be a toned-down version relative to Trump because he is such a caricature that no one would take it seriously as fiction.[37]

Self-deception is mainly adaptive, or it would not be part of our psyche. That's the point Trivers makes, and I agree. In fact, as I hope I've already made clear and will address one more time in the finale of this thing, dissociation is part of our dynamic response to the environment. It balances our internal and external experience in an ideal model. Understanding this system usually takes paying extra attention to both positive and negative extremes or just to extreme cases in general. This book does that, but I hope it normalizes dissociation as well. In the conclusion, let's be normal for a change.

Notes

1 Loyal D. Rue, *By the Grace of Guile: The Role of Deception in Natural History and Human Affairs* (New York: Oxford University Press, 1994); R. Bierregaard, "Birds in Mixed Company," *Natural History* 6, no. 107 (1998): 49–50; H. Kummer, "Tripartite Relations in Hamadryas Baboons," in *Machiavellian Intelligence: Social Expertise and*

the Evolution of Intellect in Monkeys, Apes and Humans, eds. Richard W. Byrne and Andrew Whiten, 113–121 (Oxford: Clarendon Press, 1988); Christophe Boesch and Hedwige Boesch, "Mental Map in Wild Chimpanzees: An Analysis of Hammer Transports for Nut Cracking," *Primates* 25, no. 2 (1984): 160–170; Gerd Gigerenzer, "The Modularity of Social Intelligence," in *Machiavellian Intelligence II: Extensions and Evaluations*, eds. Andrew Whiten and Richard W. Byrne, 264–288 (Cambridge: Cambridge University Press, 1997).

2 Richard W. Byrne and Andrew Whiten, "Machiavellian Intelligence," ibid.

3 Anne E. Russon, "Exploiting the Expertise of Others," in *Machiavellian Intelligence II*, eds. Andrew Whiten and Richard W. Byrne, 174–206 (Cambridge: Cambridge University Press, 1997).

4 Robert L. Goldstone and Benjamin C. Ashpole, "Human Foraging Behavior in a Virtual Environment," *Psychonomic Bulletin & Review* 11, no. 3 (2004): 508–514.

5 Byrne and Whiten, "Machiavellian Intelligence."

6 Richard D. Alexander, "Evolution of the Human Psyche," in *The Human Revolution: Behavioral and Biological Perspectives on the Origins of Modern Humans*, eds. Paul Mellars and Chris B. Stringer, 455–513 (Edinburgh: Edinburgh University Press, 1989).

7 L.B. Alloy and L.Y. Abramson, "Learned Helplessness, Depression, and the Illusion of Control," *Journal of Personality and Social Psychology* 42, no. 6 (1982): 1114–1126; "Judgment of Contingency in Depressed and Nondepressed Students: Sadder but Wiser?" *Journal of Experimental Psychology: General* 108, no. 4 (1979): 441–485; P.M. Lewinsohn et al., "Social Competence and Depression: The Role of Illusionary Self-Perceptions," *Journal of Abnormal Psychology* 89, no. 2 (1980): 203–212; D.G. Folks et al., "Denial: Predictor of Outcome Following Coronary Bypass Surgery," *International Journal of Psychiatry in Medicine* 18, no. 1 (1988): 57–66; J. Levine et al., "The Role of Denial in Recovery from Coronary Heart Disease," *Psychosomatic Medicine* 49, no. 2 (1987): 109–117.

8 L.D. Jamner and G.E. Schwartz, "Self-Deception Predicts Self-Report and Endurance of Pain," ibid. 48, no. 3 (1986): 211–223; Joe Tomaka, Jim Blascovich, and Robert M. Kelsey, "Effects of Self-Deception, Social Desirability, and Repressive Coping on Psychophysiological Reactivity to Stress," *Personality and Social Psychology Bulletin* 18, no. 5 (1992): 616–624.

9 R.D. Lane et al., "Inverse Relationship between Defensiveness and Lifetime Prevalence of Psychiatric Disorder," *American Journal of Psychiatry* 147, no. 5 (1990): 573–578; Harold A. Sackeim, "Self-Deception, Depression, and Self-Esteem: The Adaptive Value of Lying to Oneself," in *Empirical Studies of Psychoanalytic Theory*, ed. J. Masling, 101–157 (Hillsdale, NJ: Lawrence Erlbaum Associates, 1983); Harold A. Sackeim and R.C. Gur, "Self-Deception, Other-Deception, and Self-Reported Psychopathology," *Journal of Consulting and Clinical Psychology* 47, no. 1 (1979): 213–215; "Self-Deception, Self-Confrontation and Consciousness," in *Consciousness and Self-Regulation, Advances in Research and Theory*, eds. G.E. Schwartz and Deane H. Shapiro, 139–197 (New York: Plenum Press, 1978); Delroy L. Paulhus, "Socially Desirable Responding: The Evolution of a Construct," in *The Role of Constructs in Psychological and Educational Measurement*, eds. Henry I. Braun, Douglas N. Jackson, and David E. Wiley, 49–69 (Mahwah, NJ: Lawrence Erlbaum, 2002); Roy F. Baumeister et al., "Does High Self-Esteem Cause Better Performance, Interpersonal Success, Happiness, or Healthier Lifestyles?" *Psychological Science in the Public Interest* 4, no. 1 (2003): 1–44.

10 C.D. Londoño Sulkin, "Paths of Speech: Symbols, Sociality and Subjectivity among the Muinane of the Colombian Amazon," *Ethnologies* 25, no. 2 (2003): 173–194; Eduardo Viveiros de Castro, "Cosmological Deixis and Amerindian Perspectivism," *The Journal of the Royal Anthropological Institute* 4, no. 3 (1998): 469–488.

11 Londoño Sulkin, "Paths of Speech: Symbols, Sociality and Subjectivity among the Muinane of the Colombian Amazon."; de Castro, "Cosmological Deixis and Amerindian Perspectivism."

12 I should note that Londoño Sulkin (personal communication 2005) does not support a universal etic (or outsider/scientific) explanation for the Muinane ethos. "Perspectivism," which he introduced to me as a coherent interpretation of the system of Amazonian animism, is nevertheless, like most emic (insider/native) forms of dissociation, culturally relative. Yet perspectivism seems to fulfill the same biological imperative in shielding the mind from the stressful dissonance of trance logic.

13 E.E. Evans-Pritchard, *Witchcraft, Oracles and Magic among the Azande* (Oxford: Oxford University Press, 1937).

14 Christopher Frost, Michael Arfken, and Dylan W. Brock, "The Psychology Self-Deception as Illustrated in Literary Characters," *Janus Head* 4, no. 2 (2001), www.janushead.org/4-2/frost.cfm.

15 Andrew E. Taslitz, "Willfully Blinded: On Date Rape and Self-Deception," *Harvard Journal of Law and Gender* 28 (2005): 381–446.

16 Robert L. Trivers, "Foreward," in *The Selfish Gene*, ed. Richard Dawkins, xix–xx (New York: Oxford University Press, 1976).

17 "The Elements of a Scientific Theory of Self-Deception," *Annals of the New York Academy of Sciences*, no. 907 (2000): 114–131.

18 Robert Trivers, *Natural Selection and Social Theory: Selected Papers of Robert Trivers* (Oxford University Press, USA, 2002).

19 Trivers, "The Elements of a Scientific Theory of Self-Deception."

20 Ibid.

21 Ibid.

22 Ibid.

23 Peter B. Gray, "Evolution and Human Sexuality," *American Journal of Physical Anthropology* 152 (2013): 94–118.

24 Martie G. Haselton and David M. Buss, "Error Management Theory: A New Perspective on Biases in Cross-Sex Mind Reading," *Journal of Personality and Social Psychology* 78, no. 1 (2000): 81–91; David Dryden Henningsen and Mary Lynn Miller Henningsen, "Testing Error Management Theory: Exploring the Commitment Skepticism Bias and the Sexual Overperception Bias," *Human Communication Research* 36, no. 4 (2010): 618–634; John Maynard Smith and David Harper, *Animal Signals* (Oxford: Oxford University Press, 2003).

25 Lee Cronk and Bria Dunham, "Amounts Spent on Engagement Rings Reflect Aspects of Male and Female Mate Quality," *Human Nature* 18, no. 4 (2007): 329–333.

26 Christopher Dana Lynn, R. Nathan Pipitone, and Julian Paul Keenan, "To Thine Own Self Be False: Self-Deceptive Enhancement and Sexual Awareness Influences on Mating Success," *Evolutionary Behavioral Sciences* 8, no. 1 (2014): 109–122.

27 Delroy L. Paulhus, "Measurement and Control of Response Bias," in *Measures of Personality and Social Psychological Attitudes*, eds. J.P. Robinson, P.R. Shaver, and L.S. Wrightsman, 17–59 (San Diego, CA: Academic Press, 1991).

28 Delroy L. Paulhus and P.D. Harms, "Measuring Cognitive Ability with the Overclaiming Technique," *Intelligence* 32, no. 3 (2004): 297–314.

29 Lynn, Pipitone, and Keenan, "To Thine Own Self Be False: Self-Deceptive Enhancement and Sexual Awareness Influences on Mating Success."

30 John Cassidy, "Donald Trump's Business Failures Were Very Real," *The New Yorker*, May 10, 2019; Anthony Zurcher, "The Birth of the Obama 'Birther' Conspiracy," *BBC News* (2016), https://www.bbc.com/news/election-us-2016-37391652.

31 Emily Arrowood, "The Very Definition of Sexual Assault," *U.S. News & World Report*, October 7, 2016; Aaron Blake, "21 Times Donald Trump Has Assured Us He Respects Women," *Washington Post*, March 8, 2017.

32 Kaitlyn Schallhorn, "Trump's Nicknames for Rivals, from 'Rocket Man' to 'Crooked Hillary'," *Fox News* (2017), https://web.archive.org/web/20171115134402/http://www.foxnews.com/politics/2017/10/20/trumps-nicknames-for-rivals-from-rocket-man-to-crooked-hillary.html; Adam Shaw, "Trump Debuts New Nickname for

Biden: 'Sleepycreepy Joe'," ibid. (2019), https://www.foxnews.com/politics/trump-debuts-new-nickname-for-biden-sleepycreepy-joe; Meghann Myers, "The Space Force Is Officially the Sixth Military Branch. Here's What That Means," *Air Force Times* (2019), https://www.airforcetimes.com/news/your-military/2019/12/21/the-space-force-is-officially-the-sixth-military-branch-heres-what-that-means/.

33 Rachel Maddow, *Blowout: Corrupted Democracy, Rogue State Russia, and the Richest, Most Destructive Industry on Earth* (Random House, 2019).

34 Robert L. Trivers, *The Folly of Fools: The Logic of Deceit and Self-Deception in Human Life* (New York: Basic Books, 2011); "The Elements of a Scientific Theory of Self-Deception."

35 Associated Press, "Trump Tells Allies His Wearing a Mask Would 'Send the Wrong Message'," *NBC News* (2020), https://www.nbcnews.com/politics/donald-trump/trump-tells-allies-his-wearing-mask-would-send-wrong-message-n1202001; Johanna Read, "Here's Where Americans Can Travel Now. But Should They?" *National Geographic* (2020), https://www.nationalgeographic.com/travel/2020/07/which-countries-can-americans-safely-visit-this-summer-cvd/; Phillip Bump, "Trump Says He Has Done More by This Point Than Anybody," *Washington Post* (2017), https://www.washingtonpost.com/.

36 Benjamin Swasey, "Trump Retweets Video of Apparent Supporter Saying 'White Power'," *NPR* (2020), https://www.npr.org/sections/live-updates-protests-for-racial-justice/2020/06/28/884392576/trump-retweets-video-of-apparent-supporter-saying-white-power; Caleb Ecarma, "Of Course Trump Called Armed, Right-Wing Protestors "Very Good People"," *Vanity Fair*, May 1, 2020.

37 Adam Gaffney, "Trump Sees the Coronavirus as a Threat to His Self-Interest—Not to People," *The Guardian* (2020), https://www.theguardian.com/commentisfree/2020/mar/17/trump-sees-the-coronavirus-as-a-threat-to-his-self-interest-not-to-people.

11

CONCLUSION

It Ain't My Fault That I'm Out Here Getting Loose

In 2018, US actress Tess Holliday appeared on the cover of *Cosmopolitan* magazine in the UK. There was a firestorm of Twitter rebukes spurred by the sight of the "plus-size" tattooed actress's cover photo.[1] Attitudes toward tattooing have changed so much that little was noted about her extensive work in that regard. The self-righteously indignant Twitter commentators were upset that an "obese" person (obesity categorization is based on indices that do not distinguish between fat and muscle mass or account for healthy fat, which flaw these metrics) was featured on the cover of a fashion magazine, claiming it set a bad example for young people about eating, diet, and self-control.

A less famous incident in popular culture, but noteworthy among my academic colleagues, was a Twitter comment made in 2013 by evolutionary psychologist Geoffrey Miller stating that students who could not control their carbohydrate intake would not be able to hack it through graduate school. While Holliday, an activist and proponent of body-positivity, deliberately entered the fray—much like singing sensation Lizzo, whose scantily clad Instagram posts defy critics to comment on her size—Miller seems to have entered the public debate accidentally. He posted his Twitter comment while sitting in the audience of a keynote address at the NorthEastern Evolutionary Psychology Society meeting, the morning after talking with numerous grad students, several of whom felt he was speaking directly to them. Miller later claimed that his gaffe was a social science experiment, instead of acknowledging that he had revealed a personal bias against fatness. He is far from alone in this prejudice—overweight people are stigmatized in US culture and blamed for their weight as though it is a moral failing, leading to widespread discrimination, bullying, and abuse.[2]

DOI: 10.4324/9781003034483-11

While dissociation helps reduce awareness of conflicts in our psyches, that sometimes means we go on being prejudice in ways that we don't even realize or that may seem inconsistent with other values. Dissociation as I have described it in this book is an ancient capacity given new meaning in the human context. It is a defense against consciousness or the stress that comes with consciousness, but, as the past two chapters have explored, it is part of our innate systems. Sometimes these systems work well, but "systems" is really a strong word. Our psychic and physiologic organization is retrofitted from preexisting capacities of ancestors, and they are not necessarily as efficient as if they were designed and built from scratch. These systems can misfire or produce favorable and unfavorable results simultaneously. How we evaluate the activities of these innate systems and their psychosocial manifestations depends on our personal or historical perspectives.

One vantage on the social media reaction to Holliday and Miller's apparent swipe at those grad students is that humans have an overactive behavioral immune system response to fatness. Psychologist Mark Schaller coined the term "behavioral immune system" to describe behaviors people tend to do unconsciously to avoid disease.[3] The physiologic immune system has two subsystems: the innate and the adaptive immune systems. The innate system, dominant in most species, is responsible for the activation of defenses to identify and remove pathogens and foreign substances. It also activates adaptive immune responses, which are responsible for developing immunological memory of new pathogens. This adaptive or acquired immune set of defenses is the basis for how vaccinations work, as the body "remembers" the previous encounter and mounts an increased response when it runs into said pathogen again.[4]

This acquired immune system is very effective in general but also known to be on a hair-trigger when not developmentally tempered through periodic exposure to stressors. For instance, numerous modern allergies and autoimmune responses appear to be in part related to the highly sanitary and hygienic environments that many of us from developed countries grow up in. Allergies are overly intense reactions to minor environmental exposures, such as to dust mites.[5] The endocrine system plays a role in these interactions as well. Better known as stress, the endocrine response to perceived stress is to fight, flee, or freeze, during which physiological immune activities pause until the perceived danger passes. This fight-flight-or-freeze behavior is the analog to the physiological response of the innate and adaptive immune systems. If someone appears to be sick, humans avoid or isolate that person so as not to be contaminated or spread the contaminant. Avoidance and isolation were the primary methods of preventing contamination before the advent of germ theory and were highly effective during the thousands of years when human groups were not only relatively smaller in number compared to today but also largely nomadic. The tendency of human groups to move around seasonally enabled them to leave behind diseases or sick individuals.[6] The instinct for avoidance of sick individuals is widespread and retained in humans, even as complete avoidance of potentially sick individuals becomes more difficult.

Schaller and others have explored these responses to perceived disease vectors in, at this point, hundreds of studies that demonstrate both the activity and overactivity of the behavioral immune system and how it is reinforced through an ongoing role in evolutionary selection pressures. For instance, in experimental studies, they find that merely seeing photos of possible disease vectors, such as feces or open wounds, triggers a disgust response and primes some aspects of mating behavior, such as a strong preference for attractive faces and athletic bodies. Several studies have shown that attractiveness and health in mates seem to be more significant factors in mate choice when environmental conditions are poor.[7] Evolutionary biologists Randy Thornhill and Corey Fincher theorize that people would rather socialize with people they know when pathogen biodiversity is greater because strangers may carry unfamiliar pathogens, a theory they call the "parasite-driven wedge."[8] When there are more environmental pathogens and especially when they vary appreciably from group to group, as in places like the tropics, where there is a new deadly disease around every tree or pool of standing water, it is more important for women to choose male mates who are resilient and can help them birth and raise healthy children. The best proxies of health are facial attractiveness and bodily fitness.[9] When environmental conditions are relaxed, such external factors are less meaningful in mating decisions.

The behavioral immune system has many interesting implications. One is that food tends to vary as means to avoid pathogens. Spicier foods are preferred in high pathogen regions of the world, where hot spices serve the dual purpose of increasing the savory qualities and killing bacteria. Relatively blander foods prevail in regions with lower pathogen prevalence.[10] Another implication is that, as with autoimmune disorders, the behavioral immune system is generalized and often misfires. These systems appear to err to the side of disease avoidance, even if what they perceive as a potential contaminant is actually safe—it is better to avoid a potentially lethal disease than to worry about offending or being wrong.[11] In the case of autoimmune disease, however, the problem is that when the body misjudges the danger of invaders, it attacks itself. And a concern with the overactive behavioral immune system is that humans tend to see those who are different or disabled as disordered, dysfunctional, or disgusting. Thus, humans have tendencies to be ableist, ageist, homophobic, racist, xenophobic, classist, and fattist. And sometimes people don't just avoid but also attack.[12]

Anthropologists Alexandra Brewis and Amber Wutich have been studying fat stigma for over a decade. One of the many problems of stigmatizing people for anything is that it makes the stigmatized behavior worse, not better. Stigmatizing fatness by suggesting that overeating is a matter of self-control leads to feelings of inadequacy that negatively impact stress and self-esteem. These lead in turn to coping strategies to deal with those problems, one of which is eating. Public health initiatives that include shaming people for their behavior are based on anti-cigarette smoking campaigns that have largely turned the public against smoking and smokers. Despite successes over decades in limiting smoking, other campaigns using shame have backfired, including anti-fat campaigns. Brewis and Wutich examined a public health effort that used behavioral immune system theory to justify the use of disgust and stigmatization and found that, though disgust may help explain the attitudes easily inculcated against violators of social taboos about cleanliness, they exacerbate underlying problems violators may have, such as poverty and limited access to education or resources.[13]

Assortatively Socializing in the Tropics

One of the principles of the parasite-driven wedge model and related behavioral immune system theory is the idea that humans are more prone to assortatively socialize when threats are high. That is, when the world is dangerous, stick to your own. Strangers are scary and potentially dangerous. In the tropics, the danger is that strangers carry different parasitic diseases than we do, so it is best to stay close to home and limit contact. In 2012, Max Stein, Andrew Bishop, and I conducted a small study of this among members of the Church of God of Prophecy in Limón Province, Costa Rica. We interviewed members at nine Church of God of Prophecy locations in the province. Costa Rica is tropical, but it is considered a developed country with relatively low disease rates, making it a popular destination for tourism. Nevertheless, there are periodic outbreaks of malaria and dengue fever, and the conditions during such outbreaks are worst for native groups like the Bribrí and Cabécar, who live mostly in the Talamanca canton of Limón Province (near the tourist hub Puerto Viejo). The Bribrí and Cabécar are among the oldest native groups in the region and were there when Columbus landed in Costa Rica on his fourth voyage to the "New World." Today, these Indigenous groups are surrounded by Costa Rican Hispanics whose families settled there during the colonial period and Afro-Caribbean descendants of plantation workers brought to Costa Rica during the banana republic phase.

The Church of God of Prophecy is an evangelical Pentecostal denomination based out of Cleveland, Tennessee, varying culturally from place to place. We expected to see speaking in tongues like I observed at Pentecostal services in the US, as discussed in earlier chapters, but we only saw it a little in Costa Rica. The head pastor for the region was from the Dominican Republic and reported that it was a characteristic of Costa Ricans to be less inclined toward the exhibitionistic charismata of tongues, so church leaders adjusted their message to reduce the emphasis placed on it.

Among the Church of God of Prophecy locations were churches run and primarily attended by Afrolimonenses, Hispanolimonenses, or Indiolimonenses, as they are termed locally. Our data are incomplete, as we conducted observations and administered surveys over a few weeks one summer and have not received funding to return. However, those data provide an impression that tendencies to socialize with others outside one's self-identified ethnic group were greatest among Hispanolimonenses and Afrolimonenses and decidedly lowest among Bribrí living outside of the reservation and going to the Church of God of Prophecy. The isolation of the Bribrí on the reservation was even greater. Rates of in-group mating among each of these ethnic populations was higher than out-group mating.

Another principal of the parasite-driven wedge model is "limited dispersal" or not traveling too far from home. Among people we interviewed and ethnographic accounts of the Bribrí, there is a dramatic difference in attitudes about traveling for work between them and non-native Costa Ricans. Whereas Afrolimonense and Hispanolimonense would often travel or move to the United States to work, especially on the cruise liners that started in Miami and regularly visited Costa Rica, few Bribrí we talked with had traveled even so far as San José, the capital city of Costa Rica, which is about 70 miles from Limón.

Happiness Is More Important than Truth

The worldly among us often find the provincial attitudes of people less traveled quaint or naïve, but if those people don't know what they're missing, are they really missing anything? Psychologist Raj Raghunathan poses a similar question in a blog he writes for *Psychology Today*. In the science fiction film, *The Matrix*, Morpheus (portrayed by Laurence Fishburne) asks Neo (the Keanu Reeves character) if he would like to stay in the world he knows or to learn the truth. Viewers sympathize with Neo and want to know more, want the truth of the weirdness behind the so-called world of the film. In this case (spoiler alert), the world is weird because humans have been subjugated by artificially intelligent machines, living plugged into virtual realities that dissociate them from their external sensory inputs. Humans live in blissful ignorance of the reality around them.[14]

In real life, Raghunathan points out, most humans really do prefer the blissfulness of blindered existence to knowing all the ugly truths of the world. There are limitless problems humans in a media-saturated world are supposed to know and care about. There are hungry people everywhere. Discrimination is rampant. The earth is poisoned by persistent organic pollutants. Deforestation is leading to the extinction of all great apes and pushing us into contact with new disease vectors every year. This year's COVID-19 pandemic is last year's swine flu, Ebola, SARS, Zika, West Nile virus, Dengue, Chikungunya, etc. The opioid epidemic is still raging, and global climate change and the related wildfires, hurricanes, and other natural disasters are piling up. These on top of life's other stressors, like worrying about an exam or how to pay for a wedding or if my salary is enough (for whatever). All of the stuff is stressful, and what can I possibly do to fix it? Meanwhile, religion is among the most successful human social structures that ever evolved and, indeed, an opiate for the masses. The entertainment industry enables us to harness ourselves to virtual reality, plugging in 24/7, if we want. In research Raghunathan conducted with colleague Yaacov Trope, they shared the positive and negative effects of caffeine consumption with participants (e.g., "caffeine promotes mental alertness" versus "caffeine makes you nervous and jittery"). They found that people in a positive mood were much more interested in the negative effects and willing to process them than subjects in a bad mood. People not in great moods didn't want to hear anything they didn't already know and were more attendant to hearing about caffeine's positive effects and what they could do to improve their moods.[15]

In his recent book called *Selfie: How We Became So Self-Obsessed and What It's Doing to Us*, journalist Will Storr points out that much of what we think of as epitomizing consciousness—thinking in the abstract, planning for the future, trying to solve problems—is not what we spend most of our time doing.[16] Our animal consciousness is more prominent in our daily activities than the special human qualities that distinguish our mentation from other animals. We spend most of our days thinking, how do I feel? How can I feel better? If I go to this event, will I enjoy it? Will I want to leave? I feel anxious—what can I change to feel less anxious? Our actions follow this train of thought, seeking out things that will enhance our feelings, from the caffeinated beverage that modulates alertness to the clothes we wear so we can feel a certain way about our bodies or project a certain sense about ourselves. While these activities do involve the abstract planning that requires self-awareness and theory of mind, the application of awareness isn't as deep and philosophical as one might assume given the cultural value we place on it. This seeming superficiality is the norm; it is specifically this superficial awareness that is aided and abetted by the behavioral immune system and dissociation and which keeps us sane. We are basic social mammals in our approach and avoidance drives, as neuroscientist Antonio Damasio notes in his now classic studies of brain lesioned patients, such as those described in *The Feeling of What Happens: Body and Emotion in the Making of Consciousness*. Feelings are the internal drives that move us toward rewarding experiences and away from those that prompt fear, disgust, or dread. Emotions are the manifestations of those feelings that are visible to those around us and which we can sometimes manipulate and override via our human consciousness.[17] But we are not always aware why we feel anxious or want to avoid someone or are averse to something.

As I have mentioned by now several times in this book, psychologists, anthropologists, and others have tended to associate the dissociation concept with stressful situations or triggers, whether those are purposeful or traumatic, personal or cultural. And I have noted that stress is not necessarily a bad thing, though the vernacular use of the term seems to suggest otherwise. Stress is a response to environmental change that causes physiological deviation from homeostasis. The conceptualization of stress changed over the course of the 20th century. In the late 19th and early 20th centuries, mortality rates in most industrialized countries transitioned from being caused primarily by infectious disease to being results mainly of stress-related chronic disease. In recognizing and addressing these shifts, physiologist Walter Cannon coined the expression "fight-or-flight" in 1915 and popularized the homeostasis concept in his book *The Wisdom of the Body*. The homeostasis concept frames stress as a deviation from a steady state, whereas more recent researchers recognize that there is no one steady lifelong state. Neuroscientists Peter Sterling and Joseph Eyer coined the term "allostasis" to mean this stability through change, and their colleague Bruce McEwen has popularized it and the related concept of "allostatic load," which refers to the deleterious and accumulated impacts of chronic distress.[18]

Schaller's model of the behavioral immune system nests within the related allostasis concept, as we adjust and modify our avoidance behavior based on circumstances and previous experience. Experiments testing the behavioral immune system have found that manipulating disease perception by, for instance, showing people photos of things that elicit disgust response stimulates immunological behaviors but that these reactions vary some based on personal or family background.[19] Similarly, barraging people with stimuli (i.e., any constant and strong visual, auditory, olfactory, or tactile input) should result in enhanced dissociation to prevent overwhelming of sensory systems. Many cultural forms of trance are in fact induced by barrages of sensory stimulation, which result in dissociation and stress response—or, I would argue, as an integral part of stress response. Practitioners of these cultural forms manipulate cognitive mechanisms for habituation and dissociation via repetition and variation, using dissonant sounds, rhythms, or pitches against backdrops of other sensory input. Or they may overdrive the senses through pain or exertion. They may also invoke dissociation by undermining other defenses through oxygen, food, or sensory deprivation, or via intoxication. Even meditation can be viewed as such a deviation from homeostasis—in some practices through intense focus on one stimulus to the exclusion of others, or in others the opposite—voiding the mind of focus entirely. Both are deviations from normal conscious allostatic cognition and come easier with practice and with the development of neural coalitions dedicated to meditative pathways.

American Football (Again) and Atheists Who Believe in Santa Claus

I am not an atheist. My children are, yet they believed in Santa Claus until they were 13 years old. On the one hand, they ridiculed Christianity and smugly asserted that they felt sorry for people who believe such lies. On the other hand, they said they felt sorry for their classmates, whose parents "lie" to them and tell them Santa Claus and the Tooth Fairy are not real. I had to bite my tongue until they finally figured it all out. Now, I like to give them a hard time about it. I love and cherish my children dearly and write this as a tribute to the process of growth and development that I had the pleasure to share with them, not as a way to embarrass them. It is a great story of the power of self-deceptive dissociation and especially its developmental influence in inculcating inconsistent information that should cause serious cognitive dissonance, yet rarely does so.

I sat recently at a high school football game with an anthropology colleague and chatted about how we dissociate negative implications of our passions, interests, and daily interactions all the time. Both of us had children at the school, and it was homecoming. As anthropologists, we discussed our love of the pageantry and cultural complexity of the whole affair—from the "costumes" of the players, bands, and auxiliary and the elaborate symbols systems developed by coaches and referees to communicate plays and infractions, to the developmental skills required to play football. Meanwhile, we noted, neither of us would let our own children play American football because of the traumatic brain injury that is increasingly associated with it. Similarly, we joked about the extreme political polarization of the current US—except at a football game.

Football is popular among all walks of life in Alabama, and I know many favorite players, coaches, and owners are conservative Trump supporters. I prefer not to talk politics because I don't want to find myself biased against someone or some entity I liked. It's difficult to understand the contradictions that others apparently walk around with until we can note and observe our own. The amazing capacity of our dissociative tendencies is that we compartmentalize and assign different value and narrative meaning to our divergent thoughts and beliefs. Kids perhaps walk around with the most contradictions of all, such as being atheists who believe in Santa Claus.

On closer examination, is it any different for adults to believe in the miracles of saints or that Jesus walked on water, yet understand that superheroes are just fantasies created by comic book creators? We can hold conflicting thoughts and beliefs because we assign them differing degrees of importance. Most beliefs we don't examine deeply, nor do we analyze the contradictions or attempt to rectify the conflicts that are part and parcel of our daily activities and interactions. Our brains likely store some information in networks that never interact, so we can easily deceive ourselves—or, to put it less judgmentally, overlook inconsistencies—by storing and retrieving information from different areas of our brains in different contexts.

I hope this book has shed some light on the inherent contradictions of all our psyches and normalized what often seems exotic. I don't expect this book to change the ways we think—we've been an immensely successful species because of the psychic Rube Goldberg machine that is consciousness. We can know our own minds and, to a lesser degree, imagine the minds of others, but all that knowledge and imagination creates stress. Our ability to look at a problem from multiple viewpoints and imagine others' reactions places a great psychic burden on our choices. At times, this burden of consciousness is overwhelming, and we seek escape. When I used drugs, I was trying to ease my anxiety and erase the feeling that there was something important I was missing. Later, at 12-step drug and alcohol recovery meetings, I picked up the expression "let go and let God." This idea that we should stop worrying about things we cannot control and let God deal with it is also emphasized by Pentecostals. Let God speak on your behalf and literally through you.

Humans like to believe that our consciousness and awareness make us unique despite our very basic and generic mammalian socialness. We think of our human world and interactions as bearing no relation to that of chimps or dogs. But the biology is the same, and so the idea that we are somehow higher and enlightened beings seems rather absurd.

We seem, at least in Western society, to think that we should always be making steady progress toward some goal or achievement in order to "make something" of ourselves. For whom or to what purpose? Our searches and struggles take on the shape of the stories we are drawn to—for instance, "the hero's journey" that literature professor Joseph Campbell wrote of. Campbell believed that we search outwardly for a Holy Grail that only appears inside of us when we stop looking.[20] This search is the biolooping of our minds discussed in earlier chapters. We search unceasingly for meaning because the importance of that quest is one of the messages we get from our culture. In his final and most expansive work, cultural historian Jacques Barzun sarcastically notes (making a jab a recent researchers who claimed to have discovered this scientifically) that those who think a lot and deeply, from Aristotle to our present-day intellectuals, have always tended to be melancholic and that "[t]he structure of society exacerbates the disharmony [of mind]."[21]

But society gives us the balm for consciousness too, teaching us that there are thousands of ways to dissociate and thereby quiet our psychic turmoil. I found so many things Pentecostals say about worship reflect the folk wisdom of religion in this regard. An example for all Christians from the bible says that "idle hands are the devil's workshop; idle lips are his mouthpiece" (Proverbs 16:27–29, KJV). As much as people want to interpret this to mean that people should stay busy to keep out of trouble, it's as much a warning that staying occupied will keep us from thinking too much. It's why, as my kids grow up and need less of my mental or physical energy, I find myself putting in my ear buds to listen to a book, a podcast, or music so I can have something playing in my head other than my own thoughts as I go to the gym, walk the dog, garden, vacuum, watch football—any activity where my mind might start to tread the familiar circular path. These are the rituals and devotions that help me transcend the looping worries of growing older and being human.

Should I Save the World or Stick My Head in the Sand?

A show and book series I recently binged was *The Expanse*, in which generations of people have grown up in low-gravity space stations among an asteroid belt set up for mining the asteroids. These "Belters" chafe at the hegemonic oppression of people from Earth and Mars. Among the central characters of a crew comprising Earthlings, Martians, and Belters is a person who feels all the dilemmas of the cosmos and wrestles constantly with the weight of them, another who feels the same heaviness but wants to escape them all somehow, and another who feels none of these conflicts and needs people around him to give him moral structure and help him decide among choices that all seem simultaneously wrong and right (e.g., should I kill them?). A metaphor reiterated in the series is that no matter how far out in space humans manage to go, we travel there with our "monkey brains" and behave in ways that are completely predictable for a social mammal with limited self-awareness, an incomplete theory of others' minds, and a filtering function that enables them to act without being overly self-reflective.

In a world where the essence of human tendencies, with our millions of conflicting desires and needs, can easily be found on demand on Twitter, Facebook, or other social media threads, it is a relief to find an engrossing television show or book series—a hole where I can stick my head for a while and think about, well, the exact same things, but in space. Perhaps this is why my mom prefers a nice Disney cartoon.

Notes

1 Laura Capon, "Why the Feedback to Our Tess Holliday Shoot Proves This Is the Magazine Cover We All Needed," *Cosmopolitan* (2018), https://www.cosmopolitan.com/uk/fashion/a22872539/tess-holliday-cosmopolitan-magazine-cover-uk/.

2 Lauren Ingeno, "Fat Shaming Professor Faces Censure," *Inside Higher Ed* (2013), https://www.insidehighered.com/news/2013/08/07/fat-shaming-professor-faces-censure-university.

3 Mark Schaller, "The Behavioural Immune System and the Psychology of Human Sociality," *Philosophical Transactions of the Royal Society B: Biological Sciences* 366, no. 1583 (2011): 3418–3426.

4 Michael P. Muehlenbein, "Evolutionary Medicine, Immunity, and Infectious Disease," in *Human Evolutionary Biology*, ed. Michael P. Muehlenbein, 459–490 (Cambridge: Cambridge University Press, 2010).

5 Serge Morand, "Diversity and Origins of Human Infectious Diseases," in *Basics in Human Evolution*, ed. Michael P. Muehlenbein, 405–415 (Boston, MA: Academic Press, 2015); H. Okada et al., "The 'Hygiene Hypothesis' for Autoimmune and Allergic Diseases: An Update," *Clinical & Experimental Immunology* 160, no. 1 (2010): 1–9; Graham A.W. Rook, "Hygiene Hypothesis and Autoimmune Diseases," *Clinical Reviews in Allergy & Immunology* 42, no. 1 (2012): 5–15.

6 Lawrence M. Schell, "Human Health and the City," in *Urban Life: Readings in the Anthropology of the City*, eds. George Gmelch and Walter P. Zenner, 32–52 (Long Grove, IL: Waveland Press, 2002).

7 Schaller, "The Behavioural Immune System and the Psychology of Human Sociality."; Mark Schaller and Lucian Gideon Conway, "Influence of Impression-Management Goals on the Emerging Contents of Group Stereotypes: Support for a Social-Evolutionary Process," *Personality and Social Psychology Bulletin* 25, no. 7 (1999): 819–833; Mark Schaller and Damian R. Murray, "Pathogens, Personality, and Culture: Disease Prevalence Predicts Worldwide Variability in Sociosexuality, Extraversion, and Openness to Experience," *Journal of Personality and Social Psychology* 95, no. 1 (2008): 212–221; "Infectious Disease and the Creation of Culture," in *Advances in Culture and Psychology Volume 1*, eds. Michele J. Gelfand, Chi-yue Chiu, and Ying-yi Hong, 99–151 (New York: Oxford University Press, 2011); Mark Schaller, Justin Park, and Jason Faulkner, "Prehistoric Dangers and Contemporary Prejudices," *European Review of Social Psychology* 14, no. 1 (2003): 105–137.

8 Randy Thornhill and Corey L. Fincher, *The Parasite-Stress Theory of Values and Sociality: Infectious Disease, History and Human Values Worldwide* (Cham: Springer, 2014).

9 Steven W. Gangestad, Randy Thornhill, and Ronald A. Yeo, "Facial Attractiveness, Developmental Stability, and Fluctuating Asymmetry," *Ethology and Sociobiology* 15, no. 2 (1994): 73–85.

10 Paul W. Sherman and Jennifer Billing, "Darwinian Gastronomy: Why We Use Spices: Spices Taste Good Because They Are Good for Us," *Bioscience* 49, no. 6 (1999): 453–463.

11 Justin H. Park, Jason Faulkner, and Mark Schaller, "Evolved Disease-Avoidance Processes and Contemporary Anti-Social Behavior: Prejudicial Attitudes and Avoidance of People with Physical Disabilities," *Journal of Nonverbal Behavior* 27, no. 2 (2003): 65–87; Susan G. Brown, Ryan K.M. Ikeuchi, and Daniel Reed Lucas, "Collectivism/Individualism and Its Relationship to Behavioral and Physiological Immunity," *Health Psychology and Behavioral Medicine* 2, (2014): 653–664.

12 Lesley A. Duncan and Mark Schaller, "Prejudicial Attitudes toward Older Adults May Be Exaggerated When People Feel Vulnerable to Infectious Disease: Evidence and Implications," *Analyses of Social Issues and Public Policy* 9, no. 1 (2009): 97–115; Steven L. Neuberg, Douglas T. Kenrick, and Mark Schaller, "Human Threat Management Systems: Self-Protection and Disease Avoidance," *Neuroscience & Biobehavioral Reviews* 35, no. 4 (2011): 1042–1051; Park, Faulkner, and Schaller, "Evolved Disease-Avoidance

Processes and Contemporary Anti-Social Behavior: Prejudicial Attitudes and Avoidance of People with Physical Disabilities."; Justin H. Park, Mark Schaller, and Christian S. Crandall, "Pathogen-Avoidance Mechanisms and the Stigmatization of Obese People," *Evolution and Human Behavior* 28, no. 6 (2007): 410–414; Schaller and Conway, "Influence of Impression-Management Goals on the Emerging Contents of Group Stereotypes: Support for a Social-Evolutionary Process."; Mark Schaller and Steven L. Neuberg, "Intergroup Prejudices and Intergroup Conflicts," in *Foundations of Evolutionary Psychology*, eds. Charles Crawford and Dennis Krebs, 399–412 (New York: Taylor & Francis Group/Lawrence Erlbaum Associates, 2008).

13 Alexandra Brewis and Amber Wutich, "Stigma: A Biocultural Proposal for Integrating Evolutionary and Political-Economic Approaches," *American Journal of Human Biology* 32, no. 4 (2019): e23290.

14 Rajagopal Raghunathan to Sapient Nature, 22 July 2020, 2011, https://www.psychologytoday.com/us/blog/sapient-nature/201105/which-is-more-important-truth-or-happiness.

15 Rajagopal Raghunathan and Yaacov Trope, "Walking the Tightrope between Feeling Good and Being Accurate: Mood as a Resource in Processing Persuasive Messages," *Journal of Personality and Social Psychology* 83, no. 3 (2002): 510–525.

16 Will Storr, *Selfie: How the West Became Self-Obsessed* (Pan Macmillan, 2017).

17 Antonio R. Damasio, *The Feeling of What Happens: Body and Emotion in the Making of Consciousness* (New York: Harcourt Brace & Company, 1999); George J. Armelagos and Kathleen Barnes, "The Evolution of Human Disease and the Rise of Allergy: Epidemiological Transitions," *Medical Anthropology* 18, no. 2 (1999): 187–213.

18 Peter Sterling and Joseph Eyer, "Allostasis: A New Paradigm to Explain Arousal Pathology," in *Handbook of Life Stress, Cognition and Health*, eds. S. Fisher and J. Reason, 629–649 (New York: John Wiley & Sons, 1988); Walter B. Cannon, *Bodily Changes in Pain, Hunger, Fear and Rage*, (Boston: Charles T. Branford Co., 1915); Walter B. Cannon, *The Wisdom of the Body* (New York: W.W. Norton, 1939); Bruce S. McEwen and John C. Wingfield, "Allostasis and Allostatic Load," in *Encyclopedia of Stress*, ed. George R. Fink, 135–141 (New York: Academic Press, 2007).

19 Mark Schaller et al., "Mere Visual Perception of Other People's Disease Symptoms Facilitates a More Aggressive Immune Response," *Psychological Science* 21, no. 5 (2010): 649–652.

20 Robert A. Johnson, *He: Understanding Masculine Psychology* (New York: Harper & Row, 1989).

21 Jacques Barzun, *From Dawn to Decadence: 500 Years of Cultural Triumph and Defeat, 1500 to the Present* (New York: Harper Collins, 2000), p. 223.

INDEX